Texts in Computing

Volume 11

Invariants

A Generative Approach to Programming

Texts in Computing Series Editor
Ian Mackie   mackie@lix.polytechnique.fr

Invariants

A Generative Approach to Programming

Daniel Zingaro

ISBN 978-1-904987-83-3

College Publications
Scientific Director: Dov Gabbay
Managing Director: Jane Spurr
Department of Computer Science
King's College London, Strand, London WC2R 2LS, UK

http://www.collegepublications.co.uk

Original cover design by Richard Fraser
Cover produced by orchid creative   www.orchidcreative.co.uk
Printed by Lightning Source, Milton Keynes, UK

Preface

0.1 Motivation

When I was an undergraduate, I took two courses dealing with algorithm design and analysis. The first focused on a number of common algorithms, including those for finding shortest paths and spanning trees in graphs, finding substrings of larger strings, efficiently operating on sets, and the like. The tests and exams essentially involved memorizing the operation of these algorithms, then "executing" them on example data. I had little problem with this (surely this gives me some credibility).

The followup algorithms course took a different approach. In class, we went through various examples of dynamic programming, greedy heuristics, divide-and-conquer, and backtrack algorithms. There was some repeat from last time — shortest paths, string matching — but also new examples, in order to keep us interested. I felt I was ready for the exam — two hours later I can tell you I wasn't. (So much for that credibility.)

The exam asked us to come up with algorithms on the spot. The canonical examples of the various types of algorithms that were given in class were easy to understand on their own. My difficulty, though, was wondering where on Earth to start developing a **new** algorithm. In other words, it was easy to understand an algorithm that had already been constructed, but not easy to generate a new algorithm.

Engraving popular algorithms in the student's mind, as exemplified by the first course, seems all but useless to me if we are seriously trying to teach the concept of algorithm design. Students should learn these algorithms, of course, but only as a byproduct of understanding how good algorithms are designed. Teaching via examples culled from the various design techniques, on the other hand, seems like a good start. As I learned, though, this still doesn't always help: students may understand the design decisions available, but not be any closer to the solution than they otherwise would have been.

A third approach that I was introduced to in graduate school was to use invariants as an aide to proving programs correct. The idea was to come up with an algorithm for solving a problem, and then subsequently prove it via invariants and other predicates. This may help convince someone that their algorithm is correct but, alas, **which** algorithm are we speaking of? Again, we are relying on a leap of faith to generate the algorithm, and only then to prove its correctness. (You might even make the argument that, having sufficiently thought about the algorithm, there is little to gain from a formal proof anyway.)

This book uses Dijkstra-like invariants as a way to generate algorithms for solving problems. In the following chapters we show that a large class of algorithms can naturally be modelled by the use of invariants. Along the way, of course, some popular algorithms will be developed, using these same techniques. Using invariants can also directly lead to efficient **dynamic programming** solutions, showing that our techniques can help us understand this often confusing paradigm as well.

The book is intended to be used as part of a first or second course in computer programming at the university level. We therefore don't assume that sorting and searching are "obvious and beneath consideration". The algorithms are given in Java (rather than pseudocode or a specific formalism), in the hopes that students will feel more comfortable with the syntax and spend more time experimenting with the algorithms, getting immediate feedback from changes they make. While our goal is to help students systematically construct correct programs, it is still helpful to have code that can actually run; that students can modify to observe changes; and that can be adapted for the student's own purposes. We assume at least a superficial knowledge of Java syntax and operation, including the use of arrays. We give a brief introduction to Java so that the constructs used in the rest of the book are understandable, but this is by no means a Java programming book.

0.2   Why Study Algorithms?

There are at least three good reasons to study algorithm design.

First, each area of computer science has a number of algorithms central to its study. For example, when studying compilers, common algorithms include determining whether or not a given program is syntactically valid, and optimizing register usage during program execution. In graph theory, many problems boil down to traversing trees or graphs in specific ways. In numerical analysis, core algorithms often revolve around finding roots of equations, or maximizing or minimizing a function. Computer games use algorithms to make computer opponents appear intelligent, create Doppler effects and render graphics. The point is that no matter where your computer science studies take you, you can't get away from algorithms. It makes sense, then, to hone your algorithm design techniques now, setting up a platform for more specialized algorithms to stand on.

Second, when working as software developers, you will constantly be problem-solving and devising algorithms. Your "solution" may result from a small change to an existing algorithm, or require a new algorithm entirely. Regardless, a systematic method for devising and checking an algorithm is an asset in such situations. How else can you be sure that you have done the right thing.

Third, I hope you will come to agree that understanding and designing algorithms can be fun and intellectually rewarding. There is no magic going on here (at least, not once you understand an algorithm's workings), but we can still find extremely elegant solutions to what seem like complicated problems. To really appreciate this aspect of the field requires getting your feet wet.

Finally, you should study algorithms because you already have this book. It's too late; you might as well just keep reading.

0.3 Book Website

For further book information, please visit the book's website at `http://www.danielzingaro.com`. There, I will post errata, further exercises, examples and resources.

0.4 Acknowledgments

I would like to thank Dr. Emil Sekerinski for offering to class-test the material in a draft of this book. The guinea pigs were students in a second-year course in 2007/2008. Thanks also to Aws Albarghouthi and David Kelk for their in-depth suggestions and comments. Glenn MacEwen and Brooks Moses also provided helpful typesetting advice. Finally, thanks to College Publications for their help with the manuscript (thanks Jane!).

Contents

Chapter 1

Introduction

This chapter informally introduces the main ideas of the book. Through simple examples we illustrate the use of invariants in developing algorithms, as well as why it is important to carefully choose these invariants. We also show how invariants are natural and easily understood by their often implicit use in programs.

1.1 Why are Some Programs Correct?

Congratulations! You've landed a very lucrative job. The weight of the world is on your shoulders as you try to complete your critically important task: searching through an array, returning **true** or **false** corresponding with whether or not a given item is present in the array. It seems so easy that you feel like you're stealing money from the company.

Here's what you've done. You initialize a variable found to **false**, and start at the beginning of the array (the element at index 0), comparing elements with the target element as you traverse the array. When you find a match, found gets set to **true**. When you've gone through the whole array, you inspect found. If it is **true**, the element was present in the array; if not, the element was not present. We might write this in pseudocode as in Listing 1.1. The array we are searching is in a, found indicates whether or not the element has been found in the array, target is what we're looking for, and n is the length of the array.

Listing 1.1: Array Search Pseudocode

```
found = false;
i = 0;
while (i < n)
{
   if (a[i] == target) found = true;
   i = i + 1;
}
```

Simple. Now how do you prove to your very demanding boss that this program is correct?

The argument for the program's correctness might go as follows. Since we do not know if the target element will be present, we begin with the safe assumption that it is not. This corresponds to starting with found set to **false**. We then start at the beginning of the array, and not somewhere in the middle, because we want to "cover" all elements. If we were to start in the middle of the array and scan to the right, for instance, we might miss a match in the left half of the array. This algorithm would be incorrect. For this same reason, we want to ensure that we traverse the array to its end. When we find a match, found gets the value **true** to indicate this. At this point, further matches in the array cause innocuous assignments of **true** to found — the only thing we're doing is wasting some time scanning, even though we already know the result. The algorithm therefore always scans all elements of the array, and found always tells us if the target element is in the array.

This is a rather intuitive explanation of why the algorithm is correct. In the next section we will see that the core of this argument is not so far off from the reasoning we will do in this book.

1.2   The Role of Invariants

Invariants are properties of program segments that remain true throughout the scope to which the invariant applies. In other words, based on "where we are" in the program execution, we know if an invariant is true or not. At points where it is true, we use this to obtain knowledge of how our program is executing. If our invariant is to be true throughout the execution of a loop, we have a *loop invariant*. If our invariant is to be true over the variables of a Java class, we have a *class invariant*. In an imperative language, we may have a *module invariant*, which characterizes a property of a code module. As can be seen, there are many types of invariants — we will be restricting ourselves to loop invariants until Chapter 6.

As mentioned above, an invariant in the general case is a property that can be guaranteed to hold for a certain period of program execution. Informally (and slightly incorrectly — but keep reading), a loop invariant can be guaranteed to hold throughout the execution of a loop. Let us return to the searching example from the last section to explore this idea.

While executing inside the **while** loop, what do we know about the current state of program execution? We are looking for properties of the variables found, i, n, a and target, specifically those relating to the searching algorithm. As an example, we can state, as a loop invariant, *"the value of target is not changed"*. This is obviously true, since there are no assignments to target. (We're assuming that target was correctly set prior to this code block executing.) We most certainly want this invariant to hold, because if it didn't, we wouldn't be solving the search problem very satisfactorily at all. For example, if we were indeed allowed to change target, then assuming the array was not empty, we could just set target to the first element in the array, set found to **true**, and be finished. We assume that such obvious invariants are not to be worried about, though. If you are asked to find target in an array, and you change target before searching, the present author graciously gives up on you.

There are actually other loop invariants that are far more useless than the above. Here is such an example: "$2 + 3 = 5$". This invariant does not use any variables from our program at all — it simply states a mathematical truth. Since our program is not redefining the last few thousand years of mathematics, it is clear that it will be true throughout the execution of the loop. Again, however, it does not help us to understand the searching algorithm, and why it is correct.

To be appropriate, a loop invariant has to be true, but also say something **useful** about the algorithm that it is characterizing. To be useful in this sense will be made clear in time.

In the meantime, consider the following idea for an invariant: "found *is* **true** *if and only if the target exists among elements* a[0..i−1]". This should be intuitively satisfying, as we set found to **true** if and only if we've found the target element. Before continuing, consider whether or not this invariant is indeed true. Is it true throughout the execution of the loop?

To answer this question, let's first determine if this invariant is true *prior to* loop execution. Right before we enter the loop for the first time, we have that i = 0 and found = **false**. Do these values of the variables satisfy the invariant? They do. We can see this by splitting the invariant into its *only-if* and *if* parts, and analyzing them separately. We begin with "*if* found *is* **true** *then the target exists among elements* a[0..i−1]". This is the only-if part, which only claims something *if* found is **true**, and we know that this is not the case (because of the assignment of **false** to found above the loop). We therefore conclude that this part of the invariant is satisfied by the assignments we've made to the variables.

What about the *if* part? The "other half" of the invariant can be written as follows. "*if the target exists among elements* a[0..i−1] *then* found *is* **true**"; in other words, if we've already seen the element in our travels, then found better be **true**, or we've missed the element. We've ignored the a[0..i−1] notation until now — in fact, the only-if part of the invariant could have been anything at all, and the above reasoning would not have been disturbed. Now, however, it is important to understand this notation, which we will use to refer to the elements a[0], a[1], and so on, until a[i−1]. In other words, the notation expresses a subarray, starting with the first element and ending at the i−1st element. In general, the syntax a[l..u] refers to the elements between and including l and u in array a. Prior to loop entry, we have that i = 0. Substituting 0 for i, this part of the invariant is saying that, if our target element is in a[0..−1], then found should be **true**. Now, 0.. − 1 is an empty sum, because the second number is smaller than the first. That is, the notation a[0..−1] in this case includes elements of the array with index ≥ 0 *and* ≤ -1. No element of the array satisfies these constraints, and so there is no way that this claim can be true. We are now in the same position as for the only-if case: the *if* condition is false, so it makes no claim at all (the *then* part is immaterial), and so this part of the invariant is also true.

Let's catch our breath: what did we just do? To summarize, we made a claim about our search program in the form of an invariant, stating found would be **true** if and only if we found our target element in the first i elements of a. We then showed that this invariant is indeed true prior to executing the loop for the first time. We earlier claimed that this invariant was a *loop invariant*, though, so not only do we want it to be true right when the loop starts, but also during loop execution. In other words, when executing the loop, we continually maintain the truth of the invariant, which was established in the first place by the lines prior to the loop.

Onwards and upwards: does the loop maintain the invariant? It may not be immediately obvious, because we do not know how many times the loop will execute. If the array has 100 elements, surely we aren't expected to check that 100 iterations of the loop all preserve the invariant. Furthermore, there are loops that execute an unknown number of times — an even worse situation. The saving grace is that, to the contrary, we only require that *one* iteration of the loop maintain the loop invariant. This is because, if we show that one iteration preserves the loop invariant, then an arbitrary number of iterations must also preserve it, because the loop does the same thing on every iteration.

Let us illustrate with the current linear search example. Assuming that the invariant is true, we have to show that the two statements comprising the loop body preserve this. The statement prior to the increment of i sets found to **true** precisely when the next element in the array to visit is our target. Because of the invariant, we know that we have what we want up to and including a[i−1]. The first statement of the loop body ensures this will be true for the next element in the array as well, so after this we can increment i. We then once again have our invariant true up through a[i−1]: the target exists among this collection of elements if and only if it existed in the elements visited in the last iteration, or the one just visited in this iteration.

We now know that no matter how many iterations of the loop we perform, the invariant will always be preserved, because we showed it was true prior to the loop executing, and that it was true after one iteration. We're finally at a point to use this knowledge to claim that our search algorithm is correct — more specifically, we are in a position to show that, *if* the algorithm terminates, then it is correct. (We will return to non-termination in the next section.) To do this, we appeal to one other piece of knowledge that we have when the loop executes. Not only is the invariant true, but because the loop has stopped executing, we know that the guard of the loop (the expression after **while**) is not true. If it were true, then the loop would be executing again, and we just said that the loop was finished. If we combine the fact that i = n with the invariant by substituting n for i in the invariant, we arrive at the following: "found *is* **true** *if and only if the target exists among elements* a[0..n−1]". This is precisely the result of the algorithm that we were looking for: it says that found is **true** if and only if target has been found somewhere in the subarray a[0..n−1]. Of course, this so-called "subarray" is, at this point, the entire array, as necessary.

Note how the invariant allowed us to conclude that, upon termination, the program does what we want. This is what makes invariants useful. Invariants like $2 + 3 = 5$ are not useful because they do not help us show such properties. Also observe that we are only concerned with the truth of invariants after an iteration fully completes execution. In particular, at points corresponding to partial loop iterations, we do not require the invariant to hold. In the linear search, for example, after executing the first statement in the loop body and prior to executing the second statement, we do not care if the invariant does not hold. Thus, we can be more precise on when loop invariants must hold: prior to the first loop iteration, and after each subsequent iteration.

1.3   Not So Invariant

Let us slightly modify the above linear search to illustrate what happens in the invariant analysis with incorrect programs.

```
found = false;
i = 0;
while (i < n)
{
   i = i + 1;
   if (a[i] == target) found = true;
}
```

We've simply transposed the two lines making up the loop body. We know that the invariant is still true upon loop entry (since we haven't touched the lines prior to the loop), but is it still true after an iteration?

The current sense of foreboding hopefully convinced you that the invariant is no longer preserved — but why? We can illustrate why in a number of ways. Intuitively, what we are doing is incrementing i before checking the array element that was at index i. As a case in point, we will never check array element 0, because the first thing we do on the first iteration is increase i to 1 before consulting the array.

We can also focus on the only-if part of the invariant, which states "*if* found *is* **true** *then the target exists among elements* a[0..i−1]", and show it is not preserved. Let's say found is currently **false**, but then we increment i and set found to **true**. The target element is now at index i, and not among the indices 0..i−1. However, found is **true**! According to the invariant, this situation is illegal, as found is **true**, but the target is *not* among the elements with index 0..i−1.

Exercise 1.1   Use similar analysis to argue that the following search program is incorrect as well.

```
found = true;
i = 0;
while (i < n)
{
    if (a[i] == target) found = true;
    i = i + 1;
}
```

Exercise 1.2   Is the following search program correct? If not, show why not.

```
found = false;
i = 1;
while (i < n)
{
    if (a[i] == target) found = true;
    i = i + 1;
}
```

Exercise 1.3   Write an algorithm for this search problem that uses an array whose bounds are 5 and 22 instead of 0 and n. Give an invariant and show that it is true prior to loop execution, maintained by the loop, and allows the postcondition to be concluded.

1.4   Termination of Correct Programs

The previous sections were meant to convince you that, no matter how long the linear search program runs, the loop invariant remains true. In particular, we know that the loop invariant is true when (and if) the program terminates. Is it possible, however, that the loop does not terminate?

We are making a distinction here between what are commonly called *partial correctness* and *total correctness* of programs. If we say that a program is partially correct, it means that the invariants hold when they are supposed to, but we cannot guarantee termination of the program. A totally correct program is one which additionally terminates.

So far we only know that the above linear search example is partially correct, as we have not given an argument for termination. We can argue that it does terminate, however, as follows. The loop keeps executing only as long as i < n. So, if we can guarantee that i attains the value n, the loop will terminate at that point. What we want is for every iteration of the loop to bring us closer to this goal, for if we keep getting closer then at some point we must reach the termination state.

This sort of arguing is embodied in a quantity called the *variant*. Remember that an invariant states something about the execution of a loop that we know to be true — in other words, it is a boolean-valued function. A variant, on the other hand, is a quantity that is derived from the current state of program execution. We require its value to be decreased by each loop iteration, and also require that every state of the loop is associated with a value for the variant that is ≥ 0. If a further iteration is possible only when the variant is positive, and additionally we know that the variant decreases on every iteration, we must eventually end up in a situation where the variant is less than 0. When this happens, the loop necessarily terminates, since we know that all iterations are accompanied by positive variants.

Back to the linear search example, what can we use as a variant? Let's consider the quantity $n-i$ and determine if it meets the requirements for a variant. First, is $n - i$ decreased on each iteration of the loop? Translated into searching terms, we are asking the following. "Do we always have fewer items between i and n after an iteration as compared to before the iteration? We know this is true, simply because i is incremented. That is, if the value of our variant is $n - i$ to start an iteration, then increasing i changes it to $n - (i+1)$, which is less than $n - i$.

Next, is $n - i \geq 0$ on every possible iteration of the loop? Equivalently, is $n \geq i$? To see that it is, we appeal to the guard of the loop, which tells us that an iteration of the loop is only possible when $i < n$ or equivalently when $n > i$. In other words, we have shown that the variant is positive whenever a further iteration of the loop is possible.

You might think that there are other possible variants we could use to argue termination, instead of the one just proposed. You'd be right — the situation parallels the one we had for invariants, where we gave some rather useless invariants such as $2 + 3 = 5$. Here, we could use a contrived variant such as $(n - i) + 400$. Since we know $n - i$ is decreased on every iteration, we know that $(n - i) + 400$ is decreased as well, so our first condition on variants is maintained. Similarly, since this variant is bigger than $n - i$, we know that it takes on only positive values when the loop is about to iterate again. This variant, while valid, is entirely undesirable for the sole reason that it is not as simple as possible. It adds nothing to the termination argument, and in fact leads to confusion: why did we choose a constant 400 and not something else? (Why not the constant π, or the present author's bank account balance?) Additionally, the number of remaining iterations is obscured: the previous variant made it obvious how close we were to termination; this one not so much.

1.5   Role Reversal

At this point, you might make the argument that analyzing a simple program such as the linear search in this chapter was a fruitless endeavor, since we'd be hard pressed to get anything wrong anyway. We used invariants and variants to supplement our intuition about why the program is correct, and this is typical of the use of invariants as after-the-fact analysis. In this book, we will develop programs using the reverse of these two steps. We will first state our desired invariant, then write code that ensures it is true prior to loop entry and that it is maintained by the loop. The invariants we choose will have the property that they are easily established prior to loop entry. Furthermore, they will be useful in the sense that they will help us show that our programs act as expected.

1.6 Sneak Preview

In this chapter, we introduced the ideas about invariants, variants and loops that pervade much of what is to come. In the next chapter, we give an overview of Java as it relates to how we will use it to code and experiment with short programs. Then, in Chapter 3, we give some more examples, in the spirit of the one given here, of simple algorithms we can reason about via invariants and variants. We show that stating invariants before trying to solve the problem can give us hints of how to generate correct solutions. Chapter 4 considers searching and sorting algorithms, where we follow the same pattern of Chapter 3. In Chapter 5, we tackle dynamic programming, and show how we can apply invariants to help understand this powerful paradigm and the solutions it admits. Here, we also introduce segment tables — an intuitive technique for writing table-filling programs. Chapter 6 studies the application of loop invariants for reasoning about graph-theoretic algorithms, and introduces class invariants as a way to reason about general data abstractions. We conclude in Chapter 7 with the analysis of a larger case study involving context-free grammars.

Chapter 2

Java and Invariants

We now briefly introduce the core Java features that we use throughout the book. We also give the boilerplate for methods, which will help us argue correctness of procedures that we write. Finally, to keep things interesting, we play some games with Java that wrap up many of the chapter's lessons.

2.1   What is Java?

Java is an object-oriented language, which means that most data and procedures are contained within objects. Objects are runtime entities; they do not exist at compile-time. What exists at compile-time is the source code for classes, from which objects are created at runtime. A class is similar to a module in an imperative language (like Pascal): it defines the data that it contains and the procedures or methods which act on that data. For example, we might create a class for representing counters. At runtime, a counter is an object that can be reset to the initial value 0, or incremented by 1. The counter should not be modified in any other way; for instance, it should not be permitted for the counter to be set to an arbitrary value like 400. We can create such a class for counters in Java as in Listing 2.1.

Listing 2.1: Counter Class

```java
public class counter
{
  private int cValue;

  counter () //Constructor
  {
    cValue = 0;
  }

  public void reset ()
```

```
  {
    cValue = 0;
  }

  public void inc ()
  {
    cValue++;
  }

  public int getValue ()
  {
    return (cValue);
  }
}
```

The class has one data member cValue, which keeps track of the value of the counter. This member is marked **private**, so that its value cannot be read or modified from outside this class. Contrast that with the **public** modifiers preceding the definition of the class's methods: this indicates that they can be called from any other class. Since these methods are the only way the cValue data can be accessed or modified, we have obeyed the constraint that the counter should only be reset or incremented. The line following the declaration of cValue is an object constructor: it runs upon object initialization, giving values to variables. In this case, we begin with cValue set to 0.

Note how methods lacking a **return** statement are marked **void**, whereas methods returning data (only one here) are instead marked with the type of data they return (**int** here). Observe that constructors contain no such mark as they never return anything.

If we so desired, we could create multiple counter objects based on this class; they would all maintain their own independent counters, and calling their methods would modify or return the cValue variable associated with their object. New objects are created via the keyword **new**. We can create a counter object and access it through the variable countObj with the statement countObj = **new** counter();.

2.2   Classes Housing Procedures

The counters just described typify one use of classes: grouping data and methods together to create objects. Classes can also play a role analogous to files in imperative languages, and collect multiple, related procedures (methods) in one place. For example, we might create a class with mathematical procedures — one for determining if a number is prime, one for computing greatest common divisors, one for estimating square roots, and of course one for proving Goldbach's conjecture (send me this class, please). What's important here is that this class is not intended as an object creator; it is rather intended as a repository of global procedures that we can call. This role of classes seems to be stressed less often than the object-template role discussed above. Nevertheless, we'll use it extensively when we develop standalone procedures and argue their correctness. A primality-testing procedure should be available to test any integer; a binary search procedure should be equipped to search any array for a given value. We do not want to have to create objects just to call these methods. We can create this type of procedure with the **static** modifier, which indicates that the method is a class method that we can call independent of any instance (object) of that class.

For Java programs that run from the commandline, we'll want a facility that lets us test our code by running our procedure on some sample data. We do this by adding a main method to a class. This allows the class to act as an entry-point from which we can call other methods, perform input and output, and so on. The main method takes one argument: an array of strings representing the commandline options that the program was invoked with; we'll ignore these in this book.

To show how this works, consider Listing 2.2, where we give a simple class with two static methods: one for computing the average of two integers; the other for printing a message on the screen. We then use the main method to call these methods. Note that since the average and printMsg methods are **static**, we don't have to create any objects to access them.

Listing 2.2: Static Methods

```
class samplestatic
{

   public static double average (double a, double b)
   {
      return ((a + b) / 2);
   }

   public static void printMsg ()
   {
      System.out.println ("Hi, world!");
   }

   public static void main (String[] args)
   {
      System.out.println (average (3, 5));
      printMsg ();
   }
}
```

We often use the main method to give a test case, or receive input, on which to run an algorithm. This is by no means a test to convince us of correctness (that's what everything else in the book is for!). Instead, it is meant to show a typical call of the algorithm and the way in which it returns its result.

2.3 Input and Output

We saw in the last example that System.out has a println method that can be used to print strings and integers. The println method is in fact overloaded to output other types of object data as well, such as characters and even objects themselves. For getting input from the user, the situation is slightly more complicated. There is an analogous System.in object, which is of type InputStream. However, it provides no method for conveniently reading a line of text from the keyboard, and this is the most useful form of input for our purposes. What we do is create a BufferedReader object from System.in, which does include a method for reading an entire line of text. It stores what it has read in a string variable, so if we want to read other types of data, we can convert the string to the appropriate type before using it.

A final complication in reading data is that the readLine method of a BufferedReader object can throw an IOException; it does this when something goes wrong while reading the input. Many Java classes throw exceptions in similar situations in order to signify that something unexpected has happened. When an exception is thrown, we usually want to catch (or handle) the exception and recover from any condition that the exception is making us aware of. The alternative is to ignore the exception; we do this by not catching it, and letting it propagate back through the chain of method calls that resulted in it being thrown. If nothing catches the exception, the whole program crashes. We'll take a middle-ground approach: if an exception occurs, we handle it, but the only "handling" we do is to gracefully end the program.

Let's give an example of getting input from the keyboard and handling any exceptions that may occur. If the code block between **try** and **catch** throws an exception, it is handled by the code after **catch**. We'll show a variation of the previous example with the methods for calculating an average and printing a message, though we omit their bodies. this time, we calculate the average of two numbers entered by the user instead of two fixed values. See Listing 2.3.

Listing 2.3: Receiving Input

```
import java.io.*; //For access to BufferedReader
class sampleinput
{

    static BufferedReader br =
    new BufferedReader(new InputStreamReader(System.in));

    public static double average (double a, double b)
    //body of average

    public static void printMsg ()
    //body of printMsg

    public static void main (String[] args)
```

```
{
  String s;
  double a, b;
  printMsg ();
  System.out.print ("Enter a number: ");
  try
  {
    s = br.readLine ();
    a = Double.parseDouble (s);
  }
  catch (Exception e)
  {
    System.out.println ("Input error!");
    return;
  }

  System.out.print ("Enter a second number: ");
  try
  {
    s = br.readLine ();
    b = Double.parseDouble (s);
  }
  catch (Exception e)
  {
    System.out.println ("Input error!");
    return;
  }
  System.out.println ("Average is: " + average (a, b));
  }
}
```

Note how we print a prompt message, and then enter a **try...catch** block while we obtain input and try to convert the obtained string to a double numeric value. If any exceptions are raised inside this **try** block, they are handled in the subsequent **catch** block. In this case, the **catch** block simply tells the user he messed up, and uses **return** to terminate the program. We do this again for the second input value, and then pass both user-provided numbers to average.

2.4   Sticks and Stones

It has been too long since we mentioned invariants. (There, I feel better already!) To unify the ideas given in the introduction and the Java techniques illustrated in this chapter, we'll go through some games involving matches. (This section has absolutely nothing to do with stones; that was just my hook — and it seems to have worked on you.) The ideas used here come from [2].

The matchstick games we'll investigate go like this. There are one or more piles of matches to start with, and two players alternate taking an allowable number of matches from the piles. When it becomes a given players turn and they cannot make a valid move, that player loses and the opposing player wins. What we will do is specify one particular matchstick game and argue for an algorithm that a computer opponent can use to guarantee that he beats the human opposition.

Suppose that we have one pile of 20 matches. The allowable moves are taking one or two matches. Suppose the two opponents are named C (computer) and H (human). If C starts, his legal moves are taking 1 stick (leaving 19 on the pile) or 2 (leaving 18 on the pile); it would then be H's turn to make a move, and so on. What we are interested in is the sequence of C's moves that guarantees a win.

It's difficult to try to characterize correct moves with so many matches, so let's try for a less lofty goal: assuming C starts, how can we guarantee a win if there is just one match on the pile? This case is simple: we just remove the one match. It's then H's turn, and since there are no matches remaining, both possible moves (removing one or two matches) are invalid. We therefore have a way of winning the game starting with one match. We can say that having one match remaining is a *winning position*, because as long as we make the right moves, we can't lose no matter what the opponent does. What if we have two matches to begin with? Since a valid move is taking two matches, C can win as before. We simply take both matches, again leaving the hapless H with no move to make. Again, two matches on the pile is a winning position. If the pile starts with three matches, we are in trouble. If we take one, then H can take two and we lose; if we take two, H can take the last one and again we lose. There seems to be no way to guarantee a win starting with a pile of three matches. We call this type of position a *losing position*, because as long as our opponent makes no mistake, we can't win.

Persevering anyway, can we guarantee a win starting with four matches? In other words, is four matches a winning position for us? It is! We can argue this simply by observing what happens if we take one match. H is then left with three matches, which we know from above is a losing position. That is, no matter what H does at this point, he cannot win as long as C makes the proper moves. Starting with five matches, C can remove two matches, again leaving H with three matches and stuck in a losing position.

What if we start the pile with six matches? If we remove one match, then it becomes H's turn with five matches on the pile. Bad news: having five matches is a winning position, but this time it is H's turn so he is the one guaranteed to win if he doesn't make any mistake. If we remove two matches, then it is H's turn with four matches on the pile — another winning position for H. Six matches, therefore, is a losing position for us.

We can now start to see the emerging pattern. One and two matches are winning positions; three is a losing position. Four and five are winning positions; six is a losing position. Seven and eight are, yes, again winning positions; nine is a losing position. Following this pattern up to 20, we see that 20 is a winning position for C, assuming of course that he makes the first move.

Is 400 a winning position? While we could argue that it is by the same constructive approach as above, we can make one further observation that immediately tells us if a certain number of matches is a winning position. If the number of matches is not divisible by three, it is a winning position; otherwise, it is a losing position. The number 400 is not divisible by 3; it is therefore a winning position.

We now know that 20 is a winning position, assuming we make no mistakes in our moves. How can we make no mistakes, though? What we want is to always leave H in a losing position. If H is perpetually stuck in such a position, and we can guarantee that the game ends, then H has no way of winning. Since multiples of three matchsticks are losing positions, we want our move to remove the number of matches that results in a multiple of three matches remaining for H.

Let's see some examples. If there are 20 matchsticks to begin with, we should remove 2 matches as our move. Why? This leaves 18 for H, and 18 is divisible by 3 — a losing position. From 18, let's say that H takes two matches, leaving us with 16. Now we want to take one match as our move, leaving H at the divisible-by-three 15. Continuing in this way, H will eventually have three matches remaining, and we've already convinced ourselves that we can win from here.

We implement this game in Java, using a while-loop as the main controlling mechanism (see Listing 2.4). The invariant of the while-loop will be that the number of matches remaining is a winning position if C will make the next move, and a losing position if H will make the next move.

This is our partial correctness: if the game ends, C wins. However, the game requires input from H, so we can't easily guarantee that the game will end. H could just sit there for ever and ever (humans can be very patient if it means not being embarrassed by C) and not make his next move. We can, however, assert something more realistic: assuming that moves continue to be made, the game will eventually end. For this, we can rely on a variant. Not so long ago, we mentioned that a variant is decreased on each iteration, and that each iteration is associated with a positive value of the variant. A suitable variant in this case is the number of matches remaining. Each iteration reduces this (by one or two), and the guard of the loop forces this value to be positive when the loop is about to execute again.

Listing 2.4: Matchstick Game

```java
import java.io.*;
class matches
{

    static BufferedReader br =
```

```java
    new BufferedReader(new InputStreamReader(System.in));

public static void main (String[] args)
{
  int matches = 20;
  int turn = 1;
  int take = 0;
  String s;
  while (matches > 0)
  {
    System.out.println ("There are " + matches + ".");
    if (turn == 1)
    {
      System.out.println ("It is the computer's turn.");
      take = matches % 3;
      System.out.println ("Computer takes " + take + " matches.");
      matches -= take;
      turn = 2;
    }
    else
    {
      System.out.print ("It's your turn. Take 1 or 2 matches?");
      try
      {
        s = br.readLine ();
        take = Integer.parseInt (s);
      }
      catch (Exception e)
      {
        System.out.println ("Input error!");
        return;
      }
      if (take != 1 && take != 2)
      {
        System.out.println ("Input error!");
        return;
      }
      matches -= take;
      turn = 1;
    }
  }
  if (turn == 2)
    System.out.println ("You lose. Big surprise.");
  else
    System.out.println ("Huh? You win?");
}
}
```

2.5   Invariants as Annotations

In the previous section, we used invariants to reason about a Java program; we then created the program based on that analysis. While invariants are helpful for creating programs, they are also useful for understanding why programs are correct. In other words, the invariants we come up with during program construction are also of importance during program analysis. They can help explain loops and other constructs, which may be unclear without such comments. As a case in point, imagine reading the Java code from the previous section without the benefit of the invariants and the accompanying explanations. This lack of information would make understanding the main while-loop more time-consuming, since you would have to figure out for yourself that each iteration ensures that C is in a winning position or H is in a losing one. It is therefore helpful to maintain the invariants, variants and other annotations as comments in the code.

To demonstrate this, let's revisit the linear search example that we began the book with. This time, we'll write it as a Java method that receives an array of integers and a value as input, and returns a boolean as output, corresponding to whether or not the supplied value was found in the array. In addition to the loop annotations, it is also helpful to include *precondition* and *postcondition* information for the procedure. Preconditions are those things that must be true prior to invoking the method, but which cannot be captured via Java syntax rules. For example, one precondition of the linear search procedure is that all calls must provide an array to search, and not something else (i.e. there is no type error). However, Java is strongly typed, so we know that such a situation cannot arise. We are instead interested in any semantic constraints on the procedure that would prevent it from working properly when correctly-typed input and output parameters are given. In the linear search, we have no such constraints: any integer array and value can be given. There are no special circumstances to consider: it does not matter if the array is sorted or unsorted, empty or nonempty, containing the saught-after value once or a hundred times or not at all; the procedure will always "work". Preconditions for procedures will be given in a comment beginning with the word *Requires*.

Postcondition information, on the other hand, captures what we know to be true when the procedure finishes execution. In the case of linear search, we know that the procedure returns **true** if the value is in the array and **false** otherwise. We include postcondition information in a comment beginning with the word *Effects*.

The inclusion of pre- and post-condition information, and the inclusion of invariant and variant information, serve two distinct but complementary goals. The pre- and post-condition information serves the purpose of understanding how to use a procedure: abide by the preconditions (if any) and you are rewarded with the postconditions. The invariant and variant information provided for any contained loops are not necessary to use a procedure. However, to understand what is going on inside the procedure, we know that invariants and variants are very useful. The Java version of the linear search, exemplifying the ideas about annotations, is in Listing 2.5.

Listing 2.5: Java Linear Search

```java
class linear1
{

    static boolean search (int[] a, int value)
    {
        //Effects: returns true if and only if value is in a
        boolean found = false;
        int i = 0;
        while (i < a.length)
        {
            //Invariant: found is true if and only iff value is in a[0..i-1]
            //Variant: a.length - i
            if (a[i] == value) found = true;
            i = i + 1;
        }
        return (found);
    }
}
```

Exercise 2.1   Add precondition, postcondition and invariant information to the matchstick example. Be clear on whose turn it is on each iteration.

2.6   Pouring Water

Let's end this chapter with a little logic puzzle. We will write a Java program that interactively helps the user solve the problem, maintaining a loop invariant so that the conditions of the game are not violated.

Imagine that you have a three-litre jar and a five-litre jar, both initially empty. You have at your disposal an infinite supply of water, and the goal is to measure out exactly four litres of water. There are six permitted moves. You may empty the three-litre jar by pouring its contents onto the floor; you may do this with the five-litre jar as well. You can also pour from the three-litre to the five-litre jar, or vice versa, but the amount poured must not overflow as you pour. Finally, you may fill up the three- or five-litre jar from the water supply.

We set this game up like the matchstick example, by letting a while-loop control the program execution. We keep looping while the required postcondition has not been achieved (i.e. we haven't measured four litres), so that when the loop terminates, we know that we have solved the puzzle.

An important invariant that we must maintain is that the amount of water in the three-litre jar is no less than 0 litres and no more than 3 litres. Similarly, the five-litre jar must contain, at all times, between 0 and 5 litres. We include these invariant annotations in the Java code.

Do all six operations preserve the invariant? The first operation puts three litres of water in the three-litre jar, and does not touch the other jar. The invariant is thus maintained: both jars have a valid amount of water after its execution. The same holds for the second operation. The third and fourth empty one jar or the other, also maintaining the invariant, because 0 litres of water is a valid amount of water in a jar.

The fifth operation is more involved. First, we calculate the total amount of water currently being held by both jars. When we pour the five-litre jar into the three-litre jar, this is the most amount of water that can then exist in the three-litre jar. However, this would not take overflow into account: remember that the three-litre jar can hold no more than three litres, or we violate the invariant. Thus, we use Math.min to store three litres, instead of any potentially larger amount. To update the five-litre jar, we rely on having stored the original number of litres in the three-litre jar. We know that the most we could have poured is the difference between this value and three. However, we also know that the five-litre jar cannot hold less than 0 litres of water. This would again violate the invariant, and would occur whenever the five-litre jar did not have enough water in it to completely fill the three-litre jar. We thus use Math.max, to store 0 instead of any smaller value. In this way, we correctly update both jars. The final operation is analogous, and the resulting Java implementation is in 2.6.

Listing 2.6: Water Pouring Game

```java
import java.io.*;
class water
{

    static BufferedReader br =
    new BufferedReader(new InputStreamReader(System.in));

    public static void main (String[] args)
    {
        int fiveL = 0, threeL = 0, choice;
        String s;
        while (!(fiveL == 4))
        {
            //Invariant: 0 <= threeL <= 3; 0 <= fiveL <= 5
            System.out.print ("The 3L jar has " + threeL + "L; ");
            System.out.println (" the 5L jar has " + fiveL + "L.");
            System.out.println ("1. Empty 3L jar. 2. Empty 5L jar.");
            System.out.println ("3. Fill 3L jar. 4. Fill 5L jar.");
            System.out.println ("5. Pour 5L to 3L. 6. Pour 3L to 5L.");
            try
            {
```

```
      s = br.readLine ();
      choice = Integer.parseInt (s);
    }
    catch (Exception e)
    {
      System.out.println ("Input error!");
      return;
    }
    if (choice < 1 || choice > 6)
    {
      System.out.println ("Input error!");
      return;
    }
    //possible moves
    if (choice == 1) threeL = 0;
    if (choice == 2) fiveL = 0;
    if (choice == 3) threeL = 3;
    if (choice == 4) fiveL = 5;
    if (choice == 5)
    {
      int combine = threeL + fiveL;
      int old = threeL;
      threeL = Math.min (3, combine);
      fiveL = Math.max (0, fiveL - (3 - old));
    }
     if (choice == 6)
    {
      int combine = threeL + fiveL;
      int old = fiveL;
      fiveL = Math.min (5, combine);
      threeL = Math.max (0, threeL - (5 - old));
    }
  }
  System.out.println ("Puzzle solved");
  }
}
```

Exercise 2.2   Find a sequence of moves to solve this puzzle.

Exercise 2.3   This program has no variant, so even with a constant stream of user input, it may not terminate. How can you impose a variant so that the game must end at some point?

Exercise 2.4   Modify the algorithm to work for jars of sizes 1 and 3 liters and a target of 2 litres in the 3-litre jar.

Chapter 3

Algorithm Development

We are now ready to go through a set of examples that exhibit the use of invariants and variants for developing correct algorithms. We'll start with some rather simple examples that you've probably seen already, such as summing and multiplying elements of an array. It's important to understand how invariants are used in this simple analysis, however, in order to have a starting point for extending the ideas to more complicated algorithms. In other words, it wouldn't hurt if, before continuing, you forget the algorithms in this chapter that you already know.

3.1   Sum and Product of an Array

Let's use our techniques to develop an algorithm which, given an integer array, computes the sum of the array's elements. For example, if an array consisting of elements {1, 3, 5, 7} is given, the output is 16. If the array is empty, there are no elements to add, so the result is 0.

When iterating through the array, we have to keep track of some kind of running total that will eventually help us find the array sum; this will be the value that the algorithm ultimately returns. Let's call this variable sum. If we additionally denote the supplied array as a, we can state our desired postcondition as "sum *is the sum of all elements of* a".

Having made the postcondition sufficiently formal, we can now look for a suitable loop invariant. The important property of loop invariants (I'll ensure you never forget this) is that, when combined with the negation of the loop guard, the invariant lets us conclude the postcondition. Stated in more conventional terms, a loop invariant is *weaker* than the postcondition, but becomes as strong as (or stronger than) the postcondition when we also know that the loop guard is false. By weaker, we mean that an invariant "says less" than its corresponding postcondition. As a simple example, the proposition $x > 3$ is weaker than $x > 4$. That is, $x > 4$ makes a stronger claim than $x > 3$: it says "hey, my number is bigger than 4!" whereas its weaker counterpart dejectedly says, "my number is only bigger than 3".

To make a loop invariant weaker than a postcondition, we start with the postcondition and do something so that we weaken its claim. There are several common ways of doing this, including removing part of it, or replacing one of its parts with a claim about a smaller range. No matter how we arrive at the invariant, it must be weak enough so that we can easily make the invariant true prior to the first loop iteration. In the current example, the postcondition says something about the sum of the entire array, so to weaken this we can say something only about part of the array. A suitable invariant, found in this way, is "sum *is the sum of the first* i *elements of* a". Using our subarray notation, we can state this invariant as "sum *is the sum of the subarray* a[0..i−1]"; this is the form we'll use. This indicates that we should maintain a variable i in addition to the variable sum.

Once a suitable invariant is obtained, there are three main steps to using it to develop a correct algorithm. These are:

- Write code to establish the invariant before loop execution

- Write a loop body that preserves the invariant and reduces the variant

- Come up with a loop guard that enables the postcondition to be achieved

Let's go through these in order. First, we have to establish the invariant prior to the first iteration of the loop. In this case, we can set both sum and i to 0. Substituting these values into the invariant, the invariant claims "*0 is the sum of the subarray* a[0..−1]"; in other words, the sum of an empty subarray is 0.

Second, we have to come up with a loop body that preserves the invariant and also gets us closer to our postcondition. If we first perform the assignment sum = sum + a[i], then we have added element a[i] to the sum, so it now represents the result of adding one more element than before. If we then increment i, we have reestablished the invariant of sum holding the sum of a[0..i−1].

Finally, we require a loop guard that causes termination in exactly the case where its negation, plus the invariant, gives us our postcondition. Denoting the length of array a as n, we want to continue looping while i < n. (Remember: arrays in Java are zero-based, so the last element is found at an index of one less than the array's length.) When the loop terminates, then, we know that i = n, and substituting n for i in the invariant tells us that "sum *is the sum of the subarray* a[0..n−1]"; this represents the whole array, and thus the postcondition. The algorithm as described is presented in Listing 3.1, although we leave the variant to you.

Listing 3.1: Summing an Array

```
class sumarray
{

  static int sum (int[] a)
  {
    //Effects: returns sum of array a
    int i, sum;
    sum = 0; i = 0;
    while (i < a.length)
    {
      //Invariant: sum is the sum of a[0..i-1]
      //Variant: hmmm
      sum = sum + a[i];
      i = i + 1;
    }
    return (sum);
  }
}
```

Exercise 3.1   What is the variant for this program? Argue that it is decreased on each iteration and that each iteration is associated with a positive variant.

Exercise 3.2   The array sum program as given adds elements starting from the beginning of the array, using an increasing counter i. Write a version that adds elements starting from the end of the array. What is the invariant and variant this time?

Exercise 3.3   Does the program work for an empty array? Why or why not?

Before someone yells at me and rips this book out of your hands, let's dwell on the third goal above: coming up with an appropriate loop guard. The idea is that, when the guard is false (and hence the loop terminates), we have to be able to convince ourselves that the postcondition is achieved. We should have enough information by using *just* the negation of the loop guard and the loop invariant. In other words, not looking at the loop at all, we should be able to convince ourselves that the postcondition has been achieved. Is this the case with the given loop invariant and loop guard?

Exercise 3.4   Well, is it?

No. The negation of the guard tells us only that i >= n. In other words, with only this information and the invariant (which does not further constrain the value of i), we do not know if the value of i is equal to n after loop termination (like we hope), or some other value that is greater than n like n+400. In this latter case, we could only conclude that sum is the sum of the valid portion of array a and somehow its next 400 elements. This really makes no sense at all. We did not run into this ridiculousness above because we argued, quite logically, that since nothing else changes the value of i after the loop guard fails, it must end at n. This uses knowledge of the loop structure, though, and we're wondering if we can be complete without relying on such information.

One way to do this is to strengthen the invariant so that it additionally puts a bound on the variable i. We can't just arbitrarily strengthen an invariant, of course; the change has to be justified by the loop that it is a part of. In our current example, we could add a new clause to the invariant that states $0 <= i <= n$. The complete invariant would then be "sum it is the sum of the subarray $a[0..i-1]$; $0 <= i <= n$". We have placed a semicolon between the two parts of the invariant corresponding to the two different pieces of information it contains. Parts of invariants are also called conjuncts, because the entire invariant is claiming the conjunction of its parts.

When we use a multi-part invariant, like this one, we have to show that *all* parts of the invariant are established before the first execution and that *all* conjuncts are preserved by one iteration of the loop, assuming that the guard and invariant were true prior to the iteration. We already know that this is all true of the first conjunct because it is our original invariant. The initialization sets i to 0, so the second conjunct is established. Knowing that $i < n$ (from the guard), we can also claim that one iteration leaves i within the prescribed bounds. This is because, by adding 1 to a value that is less than n, we arrive at a value that is less or equal to n, which is allowed by the invariant. Thus, the loop body preserves the second conjunct as well.

The fact that $i = n$ after loop termination is rather obvious, so including it in invariants isn't really helpful for program analysis. It's more helpful — in fact, it is necessary — for proving program correctness. We'll include such information in invariants from now on, but continue to give it little comment.

We have also evidently left out something that the program requires, in order to work correctly. Specifically, what happens when all of the elements in the array sum to a number so large that it is not representable by an integer? Surely we cannot maintain the loop invariant, or postcondition, in this case. There will come a time when our invariant is true, but when the next number is added to sum, it overflows and no longer contains the true sum. We could explicitly state that arrays must not sum to more than the maximum integral value in the *Requires* clause of the procedure. However, we'd still be missing the case where the array elements are so small that adding them results in an integer underflow! We could include this as well, and in this specific situation it really wouldn't hurt. We refrain from doing so in this example and throughout the book, however, for two reasons. First, with more variables come more of these boundary conditions; things quickly become unruly with three or four variables, and come to obscure what we really want to talk about. Second, it seems apparent that these types of conditions must hold on program entry, without having to explicitly state it.

Exercise 3.5   If we pass an array reference pointing to **null** instead of an actual array, what does our array summing program do? Is this something we should include in the procedure's precondition? Why or why not?

Back to business. We can easily use the array sum algorithm given above to come up with an algorithm that determines the product of an array. For example, the array $\{1, 3, 5, 7\}$ has product $1 * 3 * 5 * 7 = 105$. Who cares about invariants and variants — let's just change $+$ to $*$, change the variable sum to prod for better naming, and blast through this so we can get to more interesting stuff! See Listing 3.2 for the obvious solution.

Listing 3.2: Multiplying an Array

```
class prodarray1
{

  static int product (int[] a)
  {
    //Effects: returns product of array a
    int i, prod;
    prod = 0; i = 0;
    while (i < a.length)
    {
      //Invariant: who cares
      //Variant: doesn't matter
      prod = prod * a[i];
      i = i + 1;
    }
    return (prod);
  }
}
```

... Unfortunately, this program doesn't work.

Exercise 3.6   What does the program do? Test it with sample arrays.

The reason the program doesn't work is because we made a huge mistake leaving out the invariant and variant annotations, and didn't reason about how they are influenced by the loop. Shame on me!

Evidently, the problem lies in the initialization of variables i and prod prior to loop execution. Since prod is set to 0, no matter what we multiply it by, it will remain 0 for the duration of the loop. We are not maintaining any reasonable invariant and so the value of prod at loop termination gives us nothing.

What can we do about this? One particularly bad idea would be to initialize prod to the first element of the array, then proceed to multiply it by the remaining elements. It is a bad idea because there is no guarantee that our input array has a first element to speak of — it might be empty. So, we'd have to introduce a new if-statement to test for array emptiness and do something else in this case. What we can do instead is consider why starting with a value of 0 worked in the array sum example, but not in this product one. This comes down to the fact that 0 is the identity for addition: if we add value x to 0, no matter what x is, we get x back. In other words, starting with 0 has no effect on our summation. Of course, 0 is not the identity for multiplication: if we multiply 0 by x, we do not get x back. If instead of 0, we start the variable prod at 1, whenever we multiply it by value x, we get x back. We can then continue multiplying by the remaining array elements as expected. This also causes an empty array (product of no values) to assume a product of 1, which is as good a value as any.

Exercise 3.7   Fix the array product program given above so that it actually computes products. Give a suitable invariant and variant, and argue that the loop is correct with respect to preserving the invariant and decreasing the variant.

Exercise 3.8   Using the lessons learned in this section, write a program for finding the minimum element in an integer array. Ensure that the invariant you give is established prior to loop execution and is *really* maintained by the loop. What should be used for the minimum element of an empty array?

Exercise 3.9   Repeat the previous exercise for finding the maximum element of an array.

Exercise 3.10   Write a program that determines whether or not all elements in a given integer array are equal. Be careful to sensibly deal with empty arrays.

3.2   Multiplying without Multiplying

We can often represent more "complicated" mathematical operators by writing them in terms of other, simpler building blocks. We'll show one example here involving performing multiplication in terms of addition.

Let's try multiplying the numbers 8 and 4. Think back to your grade school days: you might recall that we can do this by adding 4 groups of 8. Starting with 0, we add 8 once to get 8. Then, we add 8 three more times, in succession, finally (and laboriously) arriving at a result of 32. We do not have to do any multiplications to perform the multiplication, and this is the algorithm we'd like to achieve.

Let's assume that we will be multiplying two positive numbers that are stored in variables x and y. For our postcondition, we want a new variable z to contain the result of multiplying x and y. Based on how we multiplied 8 and 4 above, and because you've been primed to expect this, we'll achieve the postcondition by using a loop. We know how to begin thinking about this: generalize (weaken) the postcondition to a loop invariant.

The problem — and the reason I chose this example here — is that weakening the postcondition in such a way is not as obvious as before. So far, we've been dealing with postconditions that specify a property of an entire array; we weakened this claim by stating something only about the portion of the array we have visited. Now, we have no array, only two integer variables that we eventually want to multiply.

The loop invariant we are after must characterize our current progress in achieving our goal of multiplying x and y. Beginning with 0, assume that we want to progress by continuing to add y to our progress stored in z, doing this x times. The invariant must then assert the progress we have made in this way. In other words, we want to characterize the values that z will contain throughout the loop, so that when the loop terminates, z will be the correct value.

Before we do this, let's introduce variables a and b, whose values we will initialize to x and y, respectively. We do this because we cannot modify x or y in the multiplication process, or we will lose their original values and have no way to verify that we have achieved the postcondition. Note that we haven't had to do this previously, because we had no reason to modify any of the input parameters; we could therefore assume their values were unchanged when reasoning about the postcondition. (Later, we'll introduce *Definitions* which serve a similar purpose.)

We know that after we initialize a and b, $a * b = x * y$. When we modify a or b in the loop, this will no longer be true. The plan for the body of the loop will be to add b to z a total of a times. We can therefore use a as a measure of the number of times we still have to add b to z. So, at all times, we will have that $a * b$, plus what we have already computed in z, will be $x * y$. In other words, our invariant is "$a * b + z = x * y$".

There is an unsettling aspect of this invariant that wasn't present in our previous examples: how is this thing a weakening of the postcondition? To understand how, we can observe that this invariant alone does not allow us to conclude that $z = x * y$, only that $a * b + z = x * y$. We must combine this invariant with some other piece of knowledge to give us the postcondition. This other piece of knowledge, of course, is the negation of the loop guard. If we can somehow eliminate $a * b$ from the loop invariant, we would be done.

Eliminating $a * b$ amounts to making its value 0. We can do this in a number of ways. One way is to use the following loop guard: $a > 0 \;||\; b > 0$. The loop will continue while at least one of the variables has a positive value, and so terminates when both values are 0. Since $0 * 0 = 0$, we conclude that $0 + z = x * y$, and removing the zero term gives us the postcondition.

Is it necessary to get both a and b to 0, though? Surely not! For example, if we use the guard $a > 0$, and know that $a = 0$ on loop termination, then we can conclude $0 * b + z = x * y$, or equivalently $z = x * y$. In other words, it's sufficient to end the loop when $a = 0$, regardless of the value of b. Since a will act as a counter telling us how many more times to loop, this is work we'll have to do anyway; getting b to 0 as well would just be fruitless labor. It's not that the previous loop guard was wrong in a logical sense, as long as we can write an appropriate loop to maintain the invariant; we'll return to it in Exercise 3.13 for kicks (and experience) to see how we could implement the algorithm that way too.

To summarize so far, we have the following template for our loop, where x and y are the numbers to multiply:

//Requires: $x >= 0;\, y >= 0$

```
a = x; b = y; z = 0;
while (a > 0)
{
    //Invariant: a * b + z = x * y;
    //0 <= a <= x; b = y
    //Variant: a
    BODY
}
```

We have chosen the variant of a because we intend to decrement it by one on each loop iteration. Also, all iterations are associated with a positive value of a, as can be seen by looking at the bounds given to a in the invariant. The only thing left is to fill in the loop body. If we decrement a by 1, what do we have to do to z to preserve the loop invariant? For a concrete case, consider a = 4, b = 8, and z = 16, so that a * b + z = 48. We want to decrement a by 1 and increment z by some amount so that a * b + z is *still* 48. We know that 3 * 8 + 8 + 16 = 48, so if we have z = 8 + 16, we will preserve the invariant. In other words, we want to add the value of b to z. The corresponding Java program, complete with an input-test routine, is in Listing 3.3.

Listing 3.3: Multiplying Positive Numbers

```java
import java.io.*;
class intmult
{

    static BufferedReader br =
    new BufferedReader(new InputStreamReader(System.in));

    static int mult (int x, int y)
    {
        //Requires: x >= 0; y >= 0
        //Effects: returns the product of x and y
        int a, b, z;
        a = x; b = y; z = 0;
        while (a > 0)
        {
            //Invariant: a * b + z = x * y;
            //0 <= a <= x; b = y
            // Variant: a
            a = a - 1; z = z + b;
        }
        return (z);
    }

    public static void main (String[] args)
    {
        int x, y; String s;
```

```
System.out.print ("Enter the first number: ");
try
{
  s = br.readLine ();
  x = Integer.parseInt (s);
}
catch (Exception e)
{
  System.out.println ("Input error!");
  return;
}

System.out.print ("Enter the second number: ");
try
{
  s = br.readLine ();
  y = Integer.parseInt (s);
}
catch (Exception e)
{
  System.out.println ("Input error!");
  return;
}

if (x < 0 || y < 0)
{
  System.out.println ("Numbers are not both >= 0!");
  return;
}
System.out.println (mult (x, y));
  }
}
```

Exercise 3.11 Does the current integer multiplication program work if we relax the restriction that y is a positive integer, and let it be any integer? What if we do this with x?

Exercise 3.12 Was it really necessary to introduce b as a new variable? Could we have used y instead?

Exercise 3.13 We mentioned an alternative guard that we could use to solve the problem — namely, a > 0 || b > 0. The purpose of this exercise is to develop the correct loop for such a guard.

- Create a template consisting of the initialization, loop guard and loop invariant. Can we use the same invariant as before? If not, you should use a correct invariant.

- The plan for the loop body will be to proceed as before when a > 0; in other words, decrease a to 0 without changing the value of b. Now that our guard is strengthened, we're only halfway home, because we have to decrease b to 0 as well. When a is already 0, though, we know that z has its final value, so we should decrease b without modifying anything further. In other words, once we achieve the value for z, we literally decrement b just so we can get out of the loop. Write such a loop body. Ensure that the invariant is preserved in both types of iterations!

- What is the variant for this loop? Be sure that the variant you choose is decreased on *every* iteration, not just some of them!

3.3 Intermediate Assertions

If our lives were simple, we'd be able to write a program that brought us from our precondition to our postcondition in a single step. (It would be a super-duper language where we could say, "write me a killer app".) This would let us dispense with loop invariants and variants, and hey, you wouldn't be reading this otherwise nonexistent book!

Since this is not presently how programmers work, we had to concede that a problem can rarely be solved in a single step. Instead, it often takes a loop to do the job, and so to fill the gap between pre- and post-condition, we introduced loop invariants.

We're not done, however, as on a larger scale we are left with the same problem. There are lots of programs that take more than one loop to write, of course, so a single loop invariant will hardly help us reason about our postcondition in those cases. What we are lacking so far is a technique for allowing us to make intermediate claims at important points throughout our code, telling us what we know to be true at those points. For example, assume we have a problem to solve that has no obvious solution involving a single loop. Instead, you reason that you should be able to solve it with two successive loops. When the first loop terminates, we know that its invariant holds and the negation of its guard also holds. We can use this knowledge to reason about the subsequent loop. In our source text, we'd like to add an annotation prior to the second loop that states what we know about the variables, since it can help convince us that the invariant of the second loop has been established. More generally, it can serve as a bridge connecting the two loops. Such annotations are typically written in squiggly braces. the next two subsections put this into practice.

Of course, we aren't restricted to adding such annotations between two loops; we can put them anywhere in our source code. For example, let's say that we are writing a program whose precondition is $x > 0$. (Preconditions, incidentally, are just a special form of annotation written at the top of a program function.) This tells us that as soon as this code starts executing, we can assume that $x > 0$. If we then execute a statement $x = x + 1$, we know then that $x > 1$ is true. If we then execute the statement $x = x + 2$, we know that $x > 3$ holds. We would encode this information in the source as follows.

```
//Requires: x > 0
x = x + 1;
//{x > 1}
x = x + 2;
//{x > 3}
```

We don't mean to overdocument our code with annotations that seem obvious, however, and that is exactly what we did here. Anyone sufficiently familiar with thinking about programs as logical entities can tell, without the squigglies, that x attains values in specific ranges throughout the execution. We instead want to document assertions at important points in the program which help us reason about future execution; for instance, future loops, if-statements or other annotations.

3.3.1   Multiplying Negative Numbers

Let's go back to the program that multiplied two positive integers using addition. What do we have to do to make it work for any integers x and y, positive or negative? We can understand this in two steps.

First, I tricked you. The original program actually works for *any* value for y, including negative ones. Relaxing the restriction on y in this way obviously does not affect the properties of the variant we have chosen, since it deals with a only. It also leaves the invariant intact, since it doesn't matter if we continually add a positive y or a negative one to z: we still get the number of y's that correspond to the number of times we have looped.

Now, let's weaken the precondition further, allowing any integer value for x as well. We immediately cause a problem if we naively do so. For example, consider x having a value of -4. When we get to the while loop, the guard will be false and we will not execute any iterations inside the loop. We still have our invariant that holds upon loop termination, but since a is no longer constrained to be 0, we cannot conclude that z holds the product of our numbers. This should make sense, if for no other reason than that we did nothing to earn this.

The solution we adopt is to pretend that x is positive throughout the while loop. This slightly changes our invariant, which now states "a $*$ b $+$ z $=$ abs (x) $*$ y"; in other words, it is the positive value of x times whatever y is. At the end of the while-loop, then, we still have some work to do to arrive at x $*$ y. To typify the use of intermediate assertions, we leave the explanation of this to the Java implementation in Listing 3.4.

Listing 3.4: Multiplying Arbitrary Integers

```java
import java.io.*;
class intmult2
{

    static BufferedReader br =
    new BufferedReader(new InputStreamReader(System.in));

    static int mult (int x, int y)
    {
        //Effects: returns the product of x and y
        int a, b, z;
        a = Math.abs(x); b = y; z = 0;
        while (a > 0)
        {
            //Invariant: a * b + z = abs(x) * y;
            //0 <= a <= abs(x); b = y
            //Variant: a
            a = a - 1; z = z + b;
        }
        //{z = abs(x) * y}
        if (x < 0)
            z = -z;
        return (z);
    }

    public static void main (String[] args)
    {
        int x, y; String s;
        System.out.print ("Enter the first number: ");
        try
        {
            s = br.readLine ();
            x = Integer.parseInt (s);
        }
        catch (Exception e)
        {
            System.out.println ("Input error!");
            return;
        }

        System.out.print ("Enter the second number: ");
        try
        {
            s = br.readLine ();
            y = Integer.parseInt (s);
        }
```

```
    catch (Exception e)
    {
        System.out.println ("Input error!");
        return;
    }
    System.out.println (mult (x, y));
    }
}
```

3.3.2 Array Rotation

Our second example for introducing intermediate annotations is a program for affecting an array rotation. We introduce what this means by example. Let's say we have an array consisting of elements $\{5, 2, 5, 9, 1, 4, 0\}$. Conceptually, we want to tape the ends together such that the 5 in the first position and 0 in the last position are adjacent. When asked to rotate n places, we shift the numbers n places to the left.

For example, with n = 1, we get as output $\{2, 5, 9, 1, 4, 0, 5\}$. With n = 2, we get $\{5, 9, 1, 4, 0, 5, 2\}$. With n = 3, we get $\{9, 1, 4, 0, 5, 2, 5\}$.

There are a few ways to understand what is happening here. First, we can consider the elements of the input array as lying on a circle, whose first element is situated in the position initially occupied by the first 5. A rotation of 1 turns the circle counterclockwise by one element, so that the initial element of the array is now 2, and the rest of the array is found by moving clockwise along the circle. If we wanted a rotation of 2, we could turn the circle counterclockwise once more, and so on. We might imagine writing a program to do this: for a rotation of n, we loop n times, moving each array element over one position (and "wrapping around the circle" when necessary). That's a lot of work!

The second way to understand array rotations leads us away from the previous inefficiency. Looking at the example that introduced this section, we can see that the number of times we want to rotate the array tells us at which position of the input array to start the output array. Let's call the input array x and the output array y. For example, consider rotating by 3, so y is $\{9, 1, 4, 0, 5, 2, 5\}$. We have started y with the contents of element 3 of x, continued to the end of x, then appended the beginning of x. In other words, with a rotation amount of k, we could create array y and fill its elements as follows.

- Loop from 0 to the length of x using variable i as a counter

- If $i + k <$ x.length, set $y[i] = x[i+k]$

- Otherwise, $i + k >=$ x.length. Set $y[i] = x[i+k-x.length]$ in this case

We keep adding elements of x to the proper place in y, as long as there are more elements in x to add. Once we reach the end of x, we have copied every element from position k and on, but not the elements to the left of position k. That is, we have to wrap around to the beginning of x and start copying from there. To do this, the third line of the above pseudocode jumps in. The first time the if-statement is false (and the first time we're required to wrap), we have i + k = x.length, which signifies that we are at the end of the array and want to start copying elements from the beginning. We subtract x.length from x.length, arriving at 0, which is exactly the first element of x we want to copy. The next time, we'll have i + k being one more than the length of x. Again, we subtract x.length and arrive at 1 — the second element. We continue in this way until the loop terminates, since at that point we have copied everything to the left of position k as well.

Exercise 3.14   Write a Java program based on this pseudocode. Give an invariant and variant for your loop. You may use informal notation for the invariant, but be clear on the portions of y that correspond to well-defined portions of x.

This isn't half bad, except that we have the auxiliary array and its corresponding waste of space. (Plus, it doesn't really make a good case for intermediate assertions, so I'd look foolish introducing the example here.) In other words, we are looking for an in-place version of the algorithm that does not require the instantiation of a new array, but is just as fast. To start, let's think of input array x as consisting of two pieces concatenated together: the first k elements, and what we'll rigorously call "everything else". Then, the contents of y when the program completes will be the concatenation of these two pieces of x, but in the opposite order. That is, y will consist first of "everything else", followed by the first k elements of x. If we first reverse the entire x array, we are halfway home: we have the two pieces of x in the right places, but their contents are in reverse to what we want. To see this, let's reverse array {1, 2, 3, 4, 5}, getting {5, 4, 3, 2, 1}. If we want a rotation of 3, we see that the last 3 elements of the reversed array are the first 3 elements of array x (good), but in the opposite order that they were initially placed (bad). Reversing just this part of the array gives us {5, 4, 1, 2, 3}. Next, if we reverse the stuff prior to the last 3 elements, we get {4, 5, 1, 2, 3}, which is the required rotation of {1, 2, 3, 4, 5} by 3 positions. That is, we have a three-step procedure for obtaining a rotation of k on array x: reverse the whole array, reverse the last k elements, reverse the first x.length − k elements. Between these steps, we can state important annotations that help convince us of the program correctness. We include these in the Java implementation of Listing 3.5.

There are two additional things to note about this implementation. First, we have used an unannotated method for reversing a portion of an array given by its endpoints. The fact that its loop has no loop invariant should, by this time, be enough to single-handedly prevent you from trying to understand its inner-workings. This is actually what I want: we'll return to this particular loop correctness in the next section; focus on the array rotation proper for now. Second, in the intermediate assertions we require referring to the original array x, but we modify the array as we go, so we lose its original value. Instead of copying it into another array just so we can refer to it, we introduce a *definitions* clause as a comment at the start of the procedure. We have two definitions, x1 and x2, corresponding to the two pieces of x that we care about. The definitions are meant to be captured at this point in the method execution, so that when x is modified, the definitions still refer to the portions of x prior to any changes.

Listing 3.5: Array Rotation

```java
import java.io.*;
class rotate
{

    public static void swap(int[] a, int x, int y)
    {
        //Requires: x and y are within bounds of a
        //Effects: swap positions x and y in a
        int temp = a[x];
        a[x] = a[y];
        a[y] = temp;
    }

    public static void reverse(int[] a, int l, int r)
    {
        //Requires: l and r are within bounds of a
        //Effects: reverse a[l..r]
        while (l < r)
        {
            swap (a, l, r);
            l++; r--;
        }
    }

    static int[] rotate (int [] x, int k)
    {
        //Requires: k >= 0; k <= x.length
        //Effects: returns array x rotated counterclockwise k times
        //Definitions: x1 = x[0..k-1]
        //x2 = x[k..x.length - 1]
        reverse(x, 0, x.length − 1);
        //{x = rev (x2) followed by rev (x1)}
        reverse(x, x.length − k, x.length − 1);
        //{x = rev (x2) followed by x1}
        reverse(x, 0, x.length − k − 1);
        //{x = x2 followed by x1}
        return (x);
    }

    public static void main (String[] args)
    {
        //Test with the running example
```

```
    int[] a = {5, 2, 5, 9, 1, 4, 0};
    a = rotate (a, 3);
    for (int i = 0; i < a.length; i++)
      System.out.println(a[i]);
  }
}
```

3.4   Reversing an Array

Breaking promises is not cool; let's argue the correctness of an array reversal like the one we saw in the previous section. Of course, the downside to not deriving its correctness along with the previous example is that you've already seen a (correct) implementation. However, sometimes we're in such a position: we're given an implementation of an algorithm, and we want to understand how it might have been derived. (The fool who posted that code without the annotations should lose his Internet privileges.)

There are two ways we can go about trying to reverse an array. As is often the case, we can simplify things if we use extra storage. We can create a new array y whose size is the same as the array x we want to reverse, and copy elements in the opposite order. The invariant would be "*the first* i *elements of* y *are the reverse of the last* i *elements of* x".

Exercise 3.15   Give a Java implementation of this version for reversing an array, including precondition, postcondition, invariant and variant.

If you peeked at the array reverse method from the last section (shame on you!), you'll realize we did something else. We did not use an extra array for storage; instead, we performed the array reverse in-place. Let's again call the original contents of the input array x and the array as we work on it y. That is, y is the same as x on procedure entry, because we haven't changed x yet. Once we make a modification to the array, x does not change (since it is defined to be the contents of the array on procedure entry), but y does (since it is defined as the array we are modifying). We can use an invariant like the following: "*the first* i *elements of* y *are the reverse of the last* i *elements of* x *and the last* i *elements of* y *are the reverse of the first* i *elements of* x". We also want to state "*the remaining elements of* y *are the same as their corresponding elements in* x".

We can understand this invariant in another way if we focus on the portions of y that we know are the correct reversed portions of x. Specifically, we have that the first i elements and the last i elements of y are correctly set. Each time we are about to increment i, then, our invariant requires that two new elements be given proper values.

The initialization of variable i that makes the invariant true prior to iteration is i = 0. That is, we claim that the first 0 elements and the last 0 elements of y have been correctly set.

Exercise 3.16   What if we initialize i to a value like -400? The invariant would then still make no claim on the values in y, but why is this still a particularly awful idea?

Knowing that the first i elements and the last i elements of y are correctly set (our invariant), we are looking for a loop body that preserves this and which also increments i, hence bringing us closer to our goal of traversing the array. The invariant requires that y[i] be the ith value from the end of x, and that the ith value from the end of y be given the value of x[i]. That is, we want y[i] = x[x.length−i] and y[x.length−i] = x[i]. Of course, we don't have the x array anymore, but luckily the elements of x we're looking for are still present in y, because we haven't modified those elements yet.

Exercise 3.17   Using these observations, write a loop body that correctly sets these elements and increments i.

The loop guard in this example is interesting. If we naively use i < y.length, we get to a point where we execute an iteration of the loop and invalidate the invariant. As an example, consider reversing the array $\{1, 2, 3, 4, 5\}$. After the first iteration with i = 0, we'd have $\{5, 2, 3, 4, 1\}$. After the second iteration with i = 1, we'd have $\{5, 4, 3, 2, 1\}$. Evidently, we're done here, but if we persevere and reverse the next two elements, we get $\{5, 4, 2, 3, 1\}$. All elements were correct, so the next iteration after we should have stopped has invalidated the invariant.

Where do we stop swapping elements, then? We want to be able to conclude that the whole array y is the reverse of array x. If we exit the loop when i = y.length / 2, the first part of the invariant tells us that the first y.length / 2 elements are correct, and that the last y.length / 2 elements are correct. As example, with an array length of 8, we know that the first 4 elements and the last 4 elements are what they are supposed to be; thus, the whole array is reversed.

Exercise 3.18   Why does this work for arrays of odd length as well?

Exercise 3.19   Give a Java implementation of this version of reversing an array, using the ideas in this section. Be sure to be explicit about preconditions, definitions (so that you can refer to the original array contents in assertions), loop invariant and variant.

Exercise 3.20   The previous section on array rotation included a method for reversing an array, using indices i and j. What is the relationship between i and j? Give an invariant and variant for this version of the procedure. Annotate the precondition, necessary definitions and postcondition.

3.5   Multiplying with Shifting

Earlier (Section 3.2), we went through one way to multiply two arbitrary numbers: successive addition. There are other interesting ways to accomplish the same thing; the one here involves crafty use of multiplying and dividing by 2 and is sometimes known as Russian Multiplication.

The observation that sets us going this time is that we can often reduce the size of one of the numbers we are multiplying so that it comes closer to 1. If we can reduce a question of multiplying two large numbers to one involving a factor of 1, we are basically done — we just take the other number as the result.

For example, let's try to multiply 4 and 12 this way. If we divide 4 by 2 and multiply 12 by 2, we can move from $4 * 12$ to $2 * 24$ and not change the answer of the multiplication — they are both 48. We have, though, reduced the first number closer to 1. If we further divide the 2 by 2, and multiply 24 by 2, we move from $2 * 24$ to $1 * 48$. Here, we immediately conclude an answer of 48, and we have done no more than multiply and divide by 2. Such multiplications and divisions can be quickly computed on a computer by performing a right- or left-shift of one bit on the binary representations of the numbers. For this reason, each multiplication and division is very fast, contributing to an efficient algorithm overall.

Adopting the notation from our previous expedition into multiplying, let's call x and y the two numbers to multiply. Again, we can start by introducing a and b containing the values of x and y, respectively. From the above example, it appears that an invariant such as "$a * b = x * y$" might work; we can then keep looping until $a = 1$, and then take b as the answer. The loop body we might try might look like this.

```
a = a / 2;
b = b * 2;
```

As usual, for arbitrary positive integers a and b, we have to show that, under the truth of the loop invariant, the loop body preserves the invariant. Unfortunately, there are some positive values of a for which this does not hold. To see this, consider the case where a is an odd number, such as when we multiply 5 by 4. Doing our "divide and multiply" stunt, we have a problem: $5/2 = 2.5$, but a is an integer variable that cannot hold such a value. If we perform integer division on a (dropping the remainder), and multiply b by 2 as always, we get $2 * 8 = 16$. We have lost our invariant property, since the product of a and b is no longer the same. In fact, we are off by a value of 4, which is the original value that b held to start this iteration. When a is odd, then, we should first "remember" that we will be off by a factor of b, and maintain this somewhere. This somewhere will be variable z, which will have a role similar to how we used it before. Introducing z as this sort of spill-off variable leads us to invariant "$a * b + z = x * y$".

We now have two different cases that affect loop execution: a even and a odd. When a is even, we divide it by 2 and multiply b by 2. We want that the loop invariant holds prior to and after loop executions of this type. That is, we want to show the truth of the following statement: if $a * b + z = x * y$, then $(a / 2) * (b * 2) + z = x * y$. (Here, we have substituted the new values of a and b into the invariant.) We've seen this to be true, since when we integer-divide an even number by 2, we lose no information and do not have to modify z at all.

The other case is when a is odd. Here, the loop additionally adds b to z, so we want the following implication to be true: if $a * b + z = x * y$, then $(a / 2) * (b * 2) + z + b = x * y$. (Again, we have substituted the new values of a, b and z in the conclusion of this statement.) This is true as well. We can see this if we note that taking an odd number a, integer-dividing it by 2 and then multiplying it by 2 gives us $a-1$. So, $(a / 2) * (2 * b) + z + b = (a - 1) * b + b + z = a * b + z$, which we know equals $x * y$ from the premise of this implication.

A Java implementation of this algorithm as described here follows. The remaining details are left as exercises, since it's no fair if I have all the fun.

Listing 3.6: Multiplying with Shifting

```java
import java.io.*;
class intmult3
{

  static BufferedReader br =
  new BufferedReader(new InputStreamReader(System.in));

  static int mult (int x, int y)
  {
    //Requires: x >= 0; y >= 0
    //Effects: returns the product of x and y
    int a, b, z;
    a = x; b = y; z = 0;
    while (a > 0)
    {
      // Invariant: a * b + z = x * y;
      //0 <= a <= x; 0 <= b <= y
      // Variant: ???
      if (a % 2 == 1) z = z + b;
      a = a / 2; b = b * 2;
    }
    return (z);
  }

  public static void main (String[] args)
  {
    int x, y; String s;
    System.out.print ("Enter the first number: ");
    try
    {
      s = br.readLine ();
```

```
      x = Integer.parseInt (s);
   }
   catch (Exception e)
   {
      System.out.println ("Input error!");
      return;
   }

   System.out.print ("Enter the second number: ");
   try
   {
      s = br.readLine ();
      y = Integer.parseInt (s);
   }
   catch (Exception e)
   {
      System.out.println ("Input error!");
      return;
   }

   if (x < 0 || y < 0)
   {
      System.out.println ("Numbers are not both >= 0!");
      return;
   }
   System.out.println (mult (x, y));
  }
}
```

Exercise 3.21   Give a suitable variant for the loop and argue that it possesses the two defining properties of variants.

Exercise 3.22   By weakening the precondition, analyze what happens when one or both of the factors to multiply is negative. If necessary, modify the program so that it can deal with any cases that it does not currently deal with.

Exercise 3.23   Is there any particular reason why we are dividing and multiplying specifically by 2? Analyze the problem solution if we divide and multiply by a factor of 3 instead. Be sure that all values of a keep the invariant intact through an iteration. Is the resulting program easier or harder to understand? Is it more or less efficient?

Perspective

This example in particular highlights an important property that loops and their invariants must possess. In the introductory chapter, we remarked that all we have to do to show that a property is invariant for a loop is to show that it is preserved by one loop iteration. We argued that, if this one iteration preserves the invariant, then we are back where we started in that the invariant is still true. We can thus execute the loop again and know that the invariant will be true again, since we showed that this was the case once already. We can extend this to an arbitrary number of iterations, concluding that they all preserve the invariant.

What we failed to take note of earlier was that we must be sure to take an *arbitrary* loop execution into account, not any specific iteration. When the loop doesn't contain any decision statements, this distinction becomes hard to make, since whatever iteration we choose ends up representing the arbitrary case. However, when we have, say, an if-statement inside of a loop, we must be careful to ensure that, no matter which iteration we choose, it maintains the loop invariant.

The informal way we were dealing with "one iteration" of a loop came back to bite us in this section. If we choose just one type of iteration, say, "a is even", then we incorrectly conclude that the loop is correct in the general case. Instead, we have to consider one arbitrary iteration, where a could be any value, even or odd.

The pattern in this section is typical of programs that use loops in nontrivial ways. Based on the values of variables, or on some other condition, we may do different things at different times. We have to ensure that, no matter what the loop does, it maintains the invariant. In general, as seen in this section, we are interested in the general implication "if the invariant is true, then based on what the loop body does to the variables, it is still true after execution". When the loop performs different actions based on some condition (such as the condition "a is odd"), we end up with two or more specific implications to prove that branch from the general one. For example, in this section, we showed that, under the invariant and the assumption that a is even, the two assignment statements in the loop preserve the invariant. Also, under the invariant and the assumption that a is odd, the three assignment statements that are executed in the loop preserve the invariant. The assignment statement of the **if** is of course only executed in the latter case; it therefore does not affect our analysis of the case where a is even. We dance to a similar-sounding song in the next section.

3.6   Longest Plateau

The program we'd like to write now is one that, given a sorted input array of integers, outputs the length of the longest plateau that was found in the array. This example was introduced in [11].

A plateau is a subarray with the property that all of its elements are equal. What does this mean? Consider the array {1, 1, 1, 2, 3, 3}. All one-element subarrays of an array are of course plateaus — they satisfy the definition in that all of their (one) elements are the same. In this case, we have six such trivial plateaus. We have three plateaus of length two – there are two (overlapping) plateaus consisting of {1, 1} and one plateau of {3, 3}. Our longest plateau, though, is of lengh three: $\{1, 1, 1\}$. The longest plateau program, given this array as input, will therefore return 3 as output.

What is the first solution method that comes to mind? We can define the postcondition of the program by referring to the input array as a, introducing a variable p and asserting "p *is the length of the longest plateau in* a". We can then weaken this by introducing variable i and claiming, as a loop invariant, "p *is the length of the longest plateau in* a[0..i−1]". When the loop terminates, we want i to have value n, where n is the array length; thus, we have our postcondition. Each loop iteration will increment i, while at the same time ensuring that the invariant remains true. Note the streamlined approach for problems of this structure: I could have copied this paragraph almost verbatim from what was presented in the section dealing with array sums and products.

How can we initialize variables i and p so as to make the invariant true prior to loop entry? As usual, we don't want to state anything about an array whose elements we haven't looked at yet, so we might start with i = 0. Now, p has to be initialized to the length of the longest plateau in a[0..−1], which is an empty subarray. We cannot have any plateaus in an empty subarray, so we can use the assignment p = 0. The knowledge we've accrued so far is captured by the following template for our algorithm.

```
i = 0; p = 0;
while (i < n)
{
    //Invariant: p is length of the longest plateau in a[0..i-1]
    //Variant: n - i
    //modify p as necessary
    i = i + 1;
}
```

We have one crucial element left to figure out: knowing that i is about to be increased, what do we have to do to p to ensure that the invariant is not broken? That is, we know that p is the length of the longest plateau up to element $i − 1$; how can we make it the length of the longest plateau up to element i so that then we may increment i? The only new plateaus we must account for are the ones not already covered by the invariant, and those are the ones that end at element i and extend leftward. All other plateaus end at elements up to and including $i − 1$, and those are already covered by the invariant.

It seems, then, that one approach for writing the loop body might go as follows. Starting from element i, move leftward in the array, counting how far we get before the array's element changes. This will be the length of the longest plateau that we have not considered in p. We can compare this value to p, storing the larger in p. Then, p will be the length of the longest plateau up through element i, so we can increase i so that it is the length of the longest plateau up through element $i − 1$ again, as desired.

Exercise 3.24   Implement this version in Java. Be careful to give correctness arguments for the inner loop as well.

This isn't half bad. Not half bad, though, doesn't mean good, so we should try to do better. (I didn't claim I was a logician.) It would be nice if we could get rid of the nested loop structure; this would make the algorithm faster and cleaner. Each time the inner loop executes, we don't know how far to the left it will have to travel before it stops (i.e. finds a new element). In the worst case, the whole array could be made up of the same element, so the inner loop would have to go all the way back to the beginning of the array every time. That is, the inner loop could take time proportional to n — the length of the array. The outer loop executes a total of n times. On average, we can say that the inner loop might examine n/2 elements, so our worst-case, cataclysmic analysis might suggest that we look at $n * (n/2) = n^2/2$ elements. This is a number proportional to the square of n; it increases much faster than n does. We would typically describe this algorithm as having a worst-case time complexity of n^2. Ideally, we'd have an algorithm that takes time linear in the size of the array.

One observation we can make is that the maximum length of a plateau can increase by at most one when considering one more element of the array. The reasoning relies again on the fact that the only new plateaus end with the new array element. If adding this one element somehow gave us a plateau that was, say, two elements longer than p, we could remove this last element and still have a plateau whose length is one larger than that stored in p. This can't happen, though, because we are now looking at the portion of the array without the new element we considered; in other words, it is the portion of the array whose longest plateau must reside in p. Remember, p doesn't lie: it's the infallible invariant!

Now we know that on each iteration, we have only two possibilities: p remains the same or it is increased by one. It remains the same if there is no plateau of length p + 1 ending at element i. If there is such a plateau, we increment p by one.

We're therefore lead to asking the question of whether there is a plateau of length p + 1 that ends at i. That is, we want to know if all elements beginning at a[i−p], up through a[i] are the same. This amounts to comparing elements a[i−p] and a[i] for equality: if they are equal, we have a plateau of length p + 1, and we increment p by one. The resulting Java implementation is in Listing 3.7.

Exercise 3.25   Wait a sec. Shouldn't we compare all the elements between a[i−p] and a[p]? How can we assume that, just because the endpoints are equal, everything inside is equal too?

Listing 3.7: Longest Plateau

class plateau
{

    static int lengthPlateau (**int**[] a)
    {
       //Effects: returns length of longest plateau in a
       int i, p;

```
    i = 0; p = 0;
    while (i < a.length)
    {
        //Invariant: p is length of longest plateau in a[0..i-1]
        //Variant: a.length - i
        if (a[i] == a[i−p])
            p++;
        i++;
    }
    return (p);
}

public static void main (String[] args)
{
    int[] a = {1, 1, 1, 2, 3, 3};
    System.out.println (lengthPlateau (a));
}
}
```

Exercise 3.26   How would you modify the program to return the starting position of the longest plateau, instead of its length? How might you return both the starting position and the length of the longest plateau?

Exercise 3.27   Write a program that counts the number of plateaus in the supplied array. What is the minimum number of plateaus that must exist in an array of length n? What is the maximum number of plateaus? Give examples of these situations occurring.

Exercise 3.28   Weaken the precondition of the program so that all equal elements of an array must appear together, but the array may not be sorted. Show that the plateau-finding algorithm is still correct.

3.6.1   From Plateaus to Crevices

What do you get when you ask for a solution to the longest plateau problem from those unfamiliar with invariants and its associated reasoning? You get something like that presented in Listing 3.8; a typical submission to my query of several freshmen who've completed their first post-secondary computer science course.

Listing 3.8: Bad Plateaus

```
class crevice
{

    int longestPlateau(int[] ints)
    {
        int[] counts = new int[ints.length];
        int j = 0;
```

```
for(int i = 0; i < ints.length; ++i)
{
  if(ints[i] > ints[i−1])
    counts[j++] = 1;
  else
    ++ counts[j];
}
int max = −1;
for(int i = 0; i < counts.length; ++i)
{
  if(counts[i] > max)
    max = counts[i];
}
return max;
}
}
```

Allow me to interject and try to make up for the serious case of invariectomy that is present here. The counts array is supposed to contain elements that count the occurrences of each value in the array. For example, if the input array is {1, 1, 1, 2, 3, 3}, counts would contain {3, 1, 2}. It is hard to be more succinct and/or precise than this, as will be evident if you try to give an invariant characterizing the contents of counts on each iteration. After we traverse the array once, we have filled counts "correctly", so that we can traverse counts and pick out its biggest element. This represents the length of the longest plateau in the array.

This code has three problems. First, it wastes memory. Second, it is inefficient. Third, it is wrong.

Exercise 3.29   Before continuing, clarify these three allegations by referring to the parts of the code that are the culprits.

On the waste-memory front, notice that this solution uses an array of counts that is completely unnecessary if we keep our previous solution in mind. In terms of inefficiency, observe that it traverses the array twice: again, we know that one traversal is enough. Finally, let's talk correctness: what does this program do when given an empty array as input? That's right; it returns −1. Apparently, the maximum length of a plateau in an empty array is −1.

We can easily remedy this last problem. By inserting a check for array emptiness prior to the second array traversal, we can immediately return 0, and then enter the following traversal loop only if the array is not empty. While this change might be easy, we know from the previous section that it is unnecessary. There is nothing inherently "special" about this special case of an empty array; in fact, we didn't even mention it until this faulty program exposed it. Often, when invariants are not used, we see this pattern of making (what look like) special cases of more concern than they are worth.

Exercise 3.30   How might you change this program to return the starting position of the longest plateau instead of the length of the longest plateau? Is it easier or harder to make this change as compared with the version we developed with invariants?

We're not done. The program is also rife with off-by-one and array subscript bounds problems. You can analyze the program further to expose these; but by now you probably get the idea.

3.7   Largest Segment Sum

Not to lull you into a false sense of security, but we're going to follow the precise pattern of the last section once again in order to develop a program to solve the Largest Segment (subarray) Sum problem [8]. Given an integer array as input, our output will be the largest sum of any contiguous set of array elements. For example, the largest such sum in the array $\{1, 2, 3, 4\}$ is $1 + 2 + 3 + 4 = 10$; the largest sum comes from the subarray consisting of the whole array. Indeed, this will hold true whenever the array contains only positive integers, since we can get a bigger sum by considering more and more elements until we have included them all. We'll use the convention that the sum of an empty subarray is 0.

Things get dicey (i.e. interesting) when the array contains some negative numbers. If we're traversing the array and come to a negative number, it is not immediately obvious if we should include this number in a potential sum, hoping that future elements will eventually counteract its negativity, or leave it out, believing that it will just make the potential sum smaller. For example, in the array $\{4, -3, 9, -5\}$, the largest sum comes from the subarray consisting of the first three elements. This subarray includes a negative element, -3, but excludes another negative element, -5. If an array consists entirely of negative elements, the best we can do is take an empty subarray to give us a maximum sum of 0. Let's start with the standard program template:

```
i = 0; s = 0;
while (i < n)
{
    //Invariant: s is the largest−sum segment in a[0..i-1]
    //Variant: n - i
    //modify s as necessary
    i = i + 1;
}
```

Now, we want to modify s, so that incrementing i will maintain the invariant. As in the plateau problem, we have new possibilities to consider before we can increment i safely. This time, the new sums to consider are those ending at element i, since all sums ending at a prior element are already covered by the invariant. The strategy is therefore to compare s with the maximum sum ending at element i, choosing the larger as s's new value.

We might try to do this in a naive way as follows. We know that the maximum sum that ends at element i is at least 0: the sum of an empty subarray. We can then continue moving left in the array (using an inner loop), considering longer and longer sums, and updating the current maximum sum every time we exceed its value. For example, consider finding the largest sum that ends at the right end of $\{4, -2, 5\}$. We start with a maximum of 0, and then consider elements in reverse. We add 5 to the current sum, obtaining $0 + 5 = 5$ as the new maximum sum. We then add -2 to the sum, arriving at $5 - 2 = 3$; since this is less than 5, we leave the maximum found so far at 5. We then consider the final element, 4, and get $3 + 4 = 7$ as the new sum. This is our biggest sum so far, so we conclude that the maximum sum ending at the right of the array is 7.

Exercise 3.31   Give a Java implementation of the maximum sum using these ideas. Be sure to give invariants and variants for both the outer and inner loops. What is the time complexity of your solution?

If we look at the execution of the inner loop, it is evident that it duplicates most of its previous work each time it executes. Every time we consider the next element in the array, the inner loop scans backwards through the whole array, even though it just did this on the previous iteration. If, in addition to the variable s, we had variable end, and we maintain "end *is the maximum sum ending at* a[i−1]", could we use it to eliminate the inner loop? If we could make end hold the correct value up through element i, we could just take the maximum of s and end as the new value for s. So, let's consider element i and determine how to modify end so that it is the largest sum ending at a[i]. We know that end is the maximum sum ending at a[i−1], so if we add a[i] to end, we should have the maximum sum ending at a[i] as necessary. This, however, is only true when the result is positive; if it is negative, then we can do better by investigating no elements at all and using 0 as the maximum sum ending at a[i]. The Java implementation is in Listing 3.9.

Exercise 3.32   Using arguments similar to those given in the Longest Plateau, argue that the new value of end is really the maximum sum ending at a[i]. That is, show that it can be no greater by arriving at a contradiction.

Listing 3.9: Largest Segment Sum

```
class largestsumseg
{

    static int largestSum (int[] a)
    {
        //Effects: returns largest sum segment in a
        int i = 0, s = 0, end = 0;
        while (i < a.length)
        {
            //Invariant: p is maximum sum segment in a[0..i-1];
            //end is the maximum sum segment ending at a[i-1]
            //Variant: a.length - i
            end = end + a[i];
            if (end < 0) end = 0;
```

```
    //{end is maximum sum segment ending at a[i]}
    if (end > s) s = end;
    i = i + 1;
  }
  return (s);
}

public static void main (String[] args)
{
  int[] a = {4, −3, 9, −5};
  System.out.println (largestSum (a));
}
}
```

Exercise 3.33   If the input is guaranteed to be sorted, can the algorithm be made more efficient? Can the invariant be weakened? Implement a new algorithm that takes advantage of this. What is the time complexity of your new algorithm?

Exercise 3.34   Solve the problem of the Minimum Segment Sum. Follow the development in this section, and make changes only where necessary.

Perspective

The only substantial difference between the development in this section and the Longest Plateau development is in re-establishing the loop invariant prior to incrementing the loop variable. In the Longest Plateau, we were able to do this by a comparison between two array elements. Here, we found it necessary to introduce a new variable, end, whose own invariant was both easy to establish and helpful for establishing the main part of the invariant.

When we study dynamic programming, we will see this general trend being extended further. Instead of requiring one additional piece of data, we may require n additional pieces, all of which may be necessary in order to re-establish the loop invariant. In some cases, we may even require more than n pieces of data; for example, data proportional to its square. The important thing is to note that this extra data should only be introduced when it helps further our main algorithmic goal. Looking for an efficient solution to the Segment Sum problem here, we introduced end; without it, we would have had to settle for a less efficient alternative. The new variable also made the program simpler, reducing two loops down to one, making it more amenable to our informal-style proofs.

3.8   A Bunch of Losers

We end this chapter with an example that brings together most of the chapter's locutions: weakening postconditions to get invariants, introducing new variables to help re-establish these invariants, and using intermediate assertions. It also exhibits the fact that coming up with invariants can be quite the intellectual challenge (i.e. great fun), especially when it is necessary to stray from the streamlined approach of previous examples.

Imagine that several candidates are vying for one position, the winner being chosen by popular vote. Voters queue up, casting their votes one at a time by speaking their candidate's name to a chairperson. After all have voted, the chairperson reports to us whether or not there is a majority winner. The question: how can the chairperson do this?

A straightforward strategy is to keep a list of the candidates' names and associated vote counts. The candidate with the biggest count at the end is the winner; we just have to check that he is a majority winner. For example, consider a vote of three candidates: Dan, Joe and Steph, all beginning with counts of 0. Assume the queue of votes given by the lined-up voters is Dan, Joe, Joe, Joe, Steph, Steph, Steph, Dan, Dan, Dan. The first voter increases Dan's count by 1, so that he has a count of 1, and Steph and Joe still have counts of 0. The next three voters cause Joe's count to be incremented three times in succession, ending at a value of 3. The next three votes similarly give Steph's count a value of 3; the final three increment Dan's count three times to a final value of 4. Dan wins (what are the odds?). However, Dan does not have more than half of the votes, so is not a majority winner.

Back to the realm of computing. This solution is relatively fast: it requires us to process all the votes just once, then search the resulting count array for the winner. It's unfortunate, though, that we are using extra memory to store these counts. If we have three candidates, our count array only has three elements; but it will have one million elements if we have one million candidates.

To arrive at the solution given in [4], we start by characterizing the postcondition. We introduce a variable cand that is to represent the candidate that has a majority in the vote, if there is one. We use array v to hold the votes, one per element; its length is n. As usual, we use i for a loop counter.

We can generalize this postcondition to an invariant: "cand *is the only possible majority winner among the votes in* v[0..i−1]". We can easily establish this truth by the assignment statements i = 0 and cand = 0. In fact, we could initialize cand to anything, since there is no possible majority winner among the first 0 votes, so the invariant claims nothing about its value.

The deficiency in this proposal is evident if we try to extend the loop invariant to cover the next array element. That is, how do we modify cand so that it is still the potential majority winner in v[0..i]? If a certain candidate is winning by a longshot in v[0..i−1], then we might be correct by keeping cand the same, no matter what the vote in v[i] is. If cand has a narrow lead on the majority, though, then what? What if two candidates are currently tied? In these cases, the vote in v[i] may well change who has the majority. We don't know anything about how much a candidate is leading by, though; only that he is leading. This is not enough information.

For a majority winner to be declared, they must earn more than half of the cast votes. In other words, at least one of the winning candidate's votes must not be offset by an opposing vote. If all votes were offset by a vote for another candidate, we could not have a majority winner, since the most votes any candidate could hope for is exactly half. To see this, imagine all voters for the winning candidate lined up on one side of a room, and all other voters on the other side. There must be at least one unmatched person from the "winning side"; all losers must have one person opposing them. We can use the number of such unmatched voters as a crucial part of a new, stronger invariant.

In addition to maintaining cand, we maintain k, the number of unmatched votes for cand. Our invariant changes to "*among the votes in* v[0..i−1] *there are* k *unmatched votes for* cand; *the remaining* i − k *votes can be paired up so that paired voters disagree*". When i = n, the only possible majority winner is cand: all votes for all other candidates are paired with a disagreeing vote, so no other candidate could have a majority.

Now we can write the loop body. Based on the vote in v[i], we have to update cand and k appropriately. If k = 0, all i current votes can be paired in such a way that each voter has an opposing voter; there is thus no winner among these votes. The vote in v[i] is thus unmatched, so we let cand = v[i] and k = 1. That is, we have one potential majority winner, the candidate voted for in v[i], who has one unmatched vote.

The other case to consider is when k is not zero, so that cand has some k unmatched votes, and is the only possible winner so far. This branch has two cases. If cand = v[i], we have yet another vote for cand. Since cand was the only possible majority winner before, and it just increased its vote count, it is still the only possible majority winner now. We thus increment k by 1, accounting for the new unmatched vote. Otherwise, v[i] doesn't equal the winner, cand. The vote in v[i], and one vote for cand, are therefore opposing. We then have only k − 1 unmatched votes for cand, so we decrement k by 1 to reestablish the invariant.

After the loop finishes executing, we have our potential majority winner in cand. To see if cand has really obtained a majority, we would have to inspect all of the votes again and ensure that cand owns more than half of them.

Exercise 3.35   How does the algorithm change if we have prior knowledge that a majority is guaranteed to exist?

The Java implementation embodying these ideas is in Listing 3.10. Instead of using candidate names, we have used integers. The test case given to the procedure uses three candidates and an arbitrary choice of votes; the winner is candidate 1.

Listing 3.10: Vote Winner

```
class winner
{
```

```
static int win (int[] v)
{
    //Effects: returns the only possible candidate with a majority;
    //if candidate i is returned, no other candidate can have a majority,
    //but it must be checked that i indeed has the majority
    int i = 0, cand = 0, k = 0;
    while (i < v.length)
    {
        //Invariant: of the votes in v[0..i-1], there are k unmatched votes for cand;
        //the remaining i - k votes can be paired up so that paired voters disagree
        //Variant: v.length - i
        if (k == 0)
        {
            cand = v[i];
            k = 1;
        }
        else
            if (v[i] == cand) k++;
            else k--;
        i++;
    }
    return (cand);
}

public static void main (String[] args)
{
    int[] v = {1, 3, 3, 3, 2, 2, 2, 1, 1, 1};
    System.out.println (win (v));
}
}
```

Exercise 3.36 Examine the following sequences of votes. Which ones have majority winners?

- {2, 2, 2, 2, 3, 4, 5, 6, 7}
- {2, 2, 2, 2, 3, 4, 5, 6, 2}
- {2, 2, 2, 2, 3, 4, 5, 6, 2, 4}
- {2}
- {2, 4}

Exercise 3.37 Complete the Java implementation so that win returns a candidate only when it is shown to be a majority (not just the majority candidate). Be sure to do something sensible when the majority candidate does not have a majority.

Chapter 4

Searching and Sorting

Searching and sorting are two of the most fundamental types of algorithms in computer science. First, they are important in everyday applications: searching staff directories, sorting football statistics, and looking up words in an electronic dictionary. Second, they are interesting in a theoretical sense because they are just complicated enough to exhibit common design techniques, but not complicated enough to be too complicated. We'll study various methods for searching and sorting in this chapter, and play some games to exhibit their use in practice.

4.1 Linear Search Theorem

In Chapter 1, we saw a method for searching an array to determine whether a given value exists in the array or not. Then, in Chapter 2, we gave a Java implementation of this. To refresh, the idea is to start at the beginning of the array, matching elements against our target element. If any element in the array was the target, we know that we found it at that point; if this never happens, the target was not in the array. The unfortunate thing about that development is that we cannot use it to assert where in the array the target was found — only that it does or does not exist.

This technique, called linear search, is actually far more widely applicable than just searching through arrays, though that is one of its main uses. In its most general form, it can be used to find the first value that meets a specified property. We'll start with an example of this, then move back to arrays and finish what we started in Chapter 1.

4.1.1 Smallest Factor

Let's devise an algorithm for finding the smallest positive factor that divides a given positive input number n. That is, given input n, we want to output i such that dividing n by i has no remainder. Since every positive integer is divisible by

1, it would be entirely uninteresting if we just returned 1 every time. Therefore, we will specifically return the smallest dividing factor that is not 1 and require that the input integer be at least 2.

For example, assume our input number is 15. We hope to return a value of 3, since 15 divides 3 with no remainder. Also, 3 is the minimum such factor: 2 does not divide 15, and we already said that 1 is not to be returned.

The idea of the linear search is to start with the first possible candidate, and work our way upwards until we meet a required condition. Intuitively, this gives us the first such candidate: if there was a lower-numbered candidate that met the condition we are seeking, we would have stopped at that point.

We can exhibit this property by formulating it as a loop invariant, then writing an appropriate loop to maintain its truth. Assume the input number is n, and we introduce counter i that keeps track of the current candidate. Our invariant will say two things. First, conjunct 1: "*no numbers in the range* [2..i−1] *divide* n". If we can form a guard that guarantees that i divides n, we would have a solution, since, by the invariant, no number less than i divides n. Next, conjunct 2 of the invariant states: "i <= n", for otherwise we might terminate the loop having produced a factor bigger than n! The current template is as follows.

```
i = 2;
while (GUARD)
{
    //Invariant: no numbers in the range [2..i-1] divide n; i <= n
    //Variant: n - i
    BODY
}
```

Turning to the guard, we want to keep searching (executing the loop) as long as we haven't found the first dividing factor. Since nothing up through i − 1 divides n (by the invariant), if i does not divide n, we still haven't met our goal and want to keep searching. This leads to a guard of !(n % i == 0). Now, inside the loop, we know that i does not divide n, so we can safely increment i by 1.

Exercise 4.1   Why can we "safely" do this? Show that it indeed preserves the first conjunct of the invariant. Show that it maintains the second conjunct of the invariant as well (hint: numbers divide themselves).

When the loop terminates, we have the negation of the guard: i is a factor of n. We also have the invariant, so that we can say something stronger: i is the smallest factor of n. The Java implementation is in Listing 4.1.

Listing 4.1: Smallest Factor

```
class linear2
{

    static int firstFactor (int n)
    {
```

```
//Requires: n >= 2
//Effects: returns first dividing factor of n
int i = 2;
while (!(n % i == 0))
{
    //Invariant: no numbers in the range [2..i-1] divide n; i <= n
    //Variant: n - i
    i = i + 1;
}
return (i);
}

public static void main (String[] args)
{
    System.out.println (firstFactor(15));
    System.out.println (firstFactor(101));
}
}
```

Exercise 4.2   What does it mean when the algorithm returns a value of n?

4.1.2 The Pattern

The linear search theorem, as exemplified in the last subsection, can be used whenever we want to find the first candidate that meets a given property. We begin with the first possible value for the candidate, which we may obtain from procedure preconditions or other applicable information. In the previous section, the starting value was 2: we require that the input number will be at least 2, so we start searching there for the first factor. The main role of the loop is to test increasing candidates, via the variable i. To do this, we use a loop guard consisting of the negation of the property we are searching for. This ensures, upon loop termination, that the negation of the guard holds. That is, the negation of the negation of our desired property holds; thus, our property holds. The loop body increments the counter by 1 to take into account the knowledge accrued from the guard. A general template for linear search may thus be stated.

```
i = first-value-of-candidate;
while (!(i does not meet property))
    i = i + 1;
```

Exercise 4.3   Write a procedure that finds the integer square root of a positive integer. The integer square root of a positive integer n is the least a such that $(a+1)^2 > n$. Be clear on your preconditions and, even though you will be using the linear search theorem, explicitly state the invariant and variant.

There is an alternate form of linear search that begins at the highest candidate instead of the lowest, working backwards instead of forwards. In this form, the loop results in giving the last candidate that meets the property, instead of the first. For example, if we use this form to solve the problem in the previous section, we might start at $n - 1$ and work down towards the number 1. The result would be the highest-numbered factor of n.

Exercise 4.4 Implement this version of the algorithm.

4.1.3 Searching an Array

We have been using linear search under the assumption that the search terminates; for example, we had a valid variant in the factor-finding algorithm. For the search to terminate, it must be possible to find a candidate that meets the property we are seeking. This will not always be the case, at which point we'll have to add information to the loop guard to ensure that it does terminate. We can see this situation if we go back to performing a search on an array. If we know that the search procedure will always be looking for an element that is present in the array, we can directly apply the template from the previous subsection to arrive at a correct program; we give a Java implementation of this in Listing 4.2. Notice that the variant is again valid: if we have not found the element so far, we must eventually find it in the portion of the array that remains. That is, the value of the variant puts an upper bound on the number of times we can still execute the loop.

Listing 4.2: Search for Existing Element

```
class linear3
{

    static int arraySearch (int[] a, int value)
    {
        //Requires: value is present in a
        //Effects: returns first position of value in a
        int i = 0;
        while (!(a[i] == value))
        {
            //Invariant: value is not in a[0..i-1]; 0 <= i <= a.length
            //Variant: a.length - i
            i = i + 1;
        }
        return (i);
    }
}
```

If we now move to the general (and realistic) case where we do not know in advance that a given element is present in the array, we are in trouble if we naively apply the linear search template. The problem, of course, is that our postcondition is too strong: it requires us to find the first location in the array where a target element exists, but there may not be such a location! In particular, if a target element doesn't exist in the array, no loop whatsoever can hope to achieve the postcondition. The code would loop again when i = a.length and try to evaluate the guard, causing a runtime exception.

Let's weaken the postcondition of the loop. The first conjunct we will assert is that "value *is not in* a[0..i−1]". Our second conjunct will be "a[i] = value *or* i = a.length". In other words, we always know that value was not missed, and that we've found the value (i < a.length) or we haven't (i = a.length).

Exercise 4.5   Why do we know that value does not exist in the array, in the case where i = a.length?

If we weaken the postcondition by eliminating the second conjunct, we can use the first conjunct as the loop invariant. Upon termination of the loop, though, we require the truth of the second conjunct as well. We therefore write the guard so that its negation gives us what we are missing from the postcondition. This way, along with the invariant, we can conclude both conjuncts of the postcondition.

Note that the second conjunct of the postcondition is in the form "a or b", stating that a or b (or both) is true. The negation of this statement — the required loop guard — should therefore be of the form (a || b). It can be written in the alternate form !(a) && !(b); this is an equivalence called DeMorgan's law.

The order of the conjuncts in the loop guard also ends up being important. Java evaluates such boolean expressions from left-to-right, and "short-circuits" the execution once it knows the result. If i has value a.length, we do not want to evaluate the other operand of the "or", since it will cause the runtime exception. If, on the other hand, the first conjunct is not true (i != a.length), we do want to evaluate the other operand to test the current array element. Once Java finds one true argument of an "or", it stops evaluating arguments, precisely what we want here. If we were to switch the order of these two conjuncts, Java would test the array index **before** ensuring that i was in bounds. The implementation is in Listing 4.3. We have chosen to reflect "value not found in the array" as a return value of −1.

Exercise 4.6   Is this a good idea? Compare and contrast this approach with throwing an exception instead of returning −1. Give such an implementation using exceptions.

Listing 4.3: Array Linear Search

```
class linear4
{

    static int arraySearch (int[] a, int value)
    {
        //Effects: returns first position of value in a,
        //or -1 if it does not exist
        int i = 0;
        while (!(i == a.length || a[i] == value))
        {
```

```
    //Invariant: value is not in a[0..i-1]; 0 <= i <= a.length
    //Variant: a.length - i
    i = i + 1;
  }
  //{value is not in a[0..i-1]; 0 <= i <= a.length;
  //a[i] = value or i = a.length}
  if (i < a.length)
    return (i);
  else
    return (-1);
  }
}
```

Exercise 4.7   Assume there are n men and n women. We refer to the men or women as the integers 0, 1, ..., n−1 (it will always be clear if we are referring to man i or woman i). Further assume that all men are married to exactly one woman (and all women are married to exactly one man — a direct result of the number of men and women being equal). A given man m feels that his marriage is *unstable* if he prefers another woman w over his wife, and w also prefers m over her current husband. (Women can feel that their marriage is unstable too, of course; we leave out this symmetric case for simplicity.) The objective is to use linear search to determine if man m feels his marriage is unstable.

The procedure you'll write, unstableMarriage, takes the following arguments.

- wifeOf: wifeOf[i] gives the man married to woman i
- husbandOf: husbandOf[i] gives the woman married to man i
- menPrefs: menPrefs[i][j] gives the jth marriage preference for man i
- womenPrefs: womenPrefs[i][j] gives the jth marriage preference for woman i
- m: the man for which we are determining instability

Note that wifeOf and husbandOf must not be contradictory: we cannot have, say, the wife of man 1 being woman 2, and the husband of woman 2 being man 3.

- In the template of Listing 4.4, there is a set of sample data in the main procedure, asking whether or not man 0 feels unstable. Does he?
- Complete the unstable procedure in Listing 4.4. There is an auxiliary procedure you may use for easing access to rankings; it is specified via pre- and post-conditions.

Listing 4.4: Stable Marriage Template

```
class marriages1
{

  public static int[][] rankMatrix (int[][] prefs)
  {
    //Requires: square array prefs, where prefs[i][j] is preference j of person i
    //Effects: returns square array ranks, where person j is
    //ranked ranks[i][j] according to i
```

```
    int[][] ranks = new int[prefs.length][prefs.length];
    for (int i = 0; i < prefs.length; i++)
    //Invariant: For rows [0..i-1] of ranks, j is ranked ranks[i][j] according to i
        for (int j = 0; j < prefs.length; j++)
            ranks[i][prefs[i][j]] = j;
    return (ranks);
}

public static boolean unstableMarriage (
    int[] wifeOf,
    int[] husbandOf,
    int[][] menPrefs,
    int[][] womenPrefs,
    int m)
    {
    //Effects: returns whether or not m views his marriage as unstable
    //BODY
}

public static void main (String[] args)
{
    //Sample data
    int[][] menPrefs =
    {{1, 2, 0},
     {0, 2, 1},
     {0, 1, 2}};

    int[][] womenPrefs =
    {{1, 2, 0},
     {0, 2, 1},
     {1, 0, 2}};

    int[] wifeOf = {2, 0, 1};
    int[] husbandOf = {1, 2, 0};
    //Does man 0 think his marriage is unstable?
    boolean res = unstableMarriage(wifeOf, husbandOf, menPrefs, womenPrefs, 0);
    System.out.println (res);
}
}
```

4.2   Binary Search

4.2.1   Guessing Numbers

Imagine you are at a really hopping party where everyone is playing Guess the
Number. One person thinks of a number between 1 and 100; the other person
tries to guess it in the minimum number of guesses possible.

Having read the last section, you know that this guessing game is rife with linear search fragrance. You start with a candidate of 1, which you know is the first possible candidate. Your "guard" is that your partner tells you that your number is incorrect. Since your "invariant" is that all numbers you have guessed so far are too low, you "increment" your number by 1 and guess the next one. If your partner's number is 83, he'll be long gone before you even get close. No one plays the game like this! What's going on?

A linear search gives us information about just one new element on each iteration. On average, then, we might expect to guess 50 numbers before we guessed correctly. If we could reduce the range of possible guesses by more than 1 at a time, we might do better. In particular, having played the game before, you know that choosing a number halfway between the bounds of your current range is a good move. It always leaves you with just half of the previous range to deal with. After one guess, we have narrowed your partner's number down to one of about 50 choices. After two guesses, we have only about 25 remaining choices, and so on.

To implement this idea, we'll write a procedure that takes a value between 1 and 100 and outputs the sequence of guesses it uses to get the number. We'll use variables i and j, coupled with the loop invariant "value *is in* [i..j]". Under the precondition, we can make the loop invariant hold if we set i = 1 and j = 100.

The guard of this loop is evident, now that the invariant is specified: we want to keep going as long as !(i == j). When the guard is false, we have i and j equal, and the invariant tells us that the number to be found is in [i..j], or exactly i. Let's summarize the current structure:

```
i = 1; j = 100;
while (!(i == j))
{
    //Invariant: value is in [i..j] and 1 <= i <= j <= 100
    //Variant: j - i
    BODY
}
```

The responsibility of the loop body is to make our next guess, and update i or j accordingly. Note that if, on each iteration, i does not increase by at least 1, or if j does not decrease by at least 1, the variant will not be decreased and we will produce an incorrect program. This has befuddled many a programmer who has tried to implement a binary search while ignoring invariants and variants; we'll come back to this.

Assume our next guess, mid, is any number in [i..j] (not necessarily the middle). There are three cases to consider. If we have found the number, we should update i and j to mid. The invariant remains true in this case, since the number is i, which is in [i..j]. Next, if mid < value, then we guessed too low. Since mid is too low, everything to the left of mid must be too low as well. The number thus lies in [mid+1..j], so we can set i = mid + 1, maintaining the invariant and decreasing the variant. Note that mid cannot be j (since j can't be too low), so that setting i = mid + 1 is guaranteed not to make i exceed j. Otherwise, we guessed too high: the number must lie in [i..mid − 1], so we set j = mid − 1. Symmetrically here, mid cannot be i.

Exercise 4.8 What if we set j = mid here instead? Is the invariant preserved? Does the variant decrease on each iteration?

Since we know that any value of mid in [i..j] is sufficient for the above correctness argument, choosing mid = (i + j) / 2, the middle of the range, should work too, as long as it really does fall in [i..j]. Consider the case where the range is [3..5]; mid will be 4: a number inside the range, as required. If the range is [3..4], then mid will be (3 + 4) / 2 = 3, again in the range (we're using integer division, of course). The quantity (i + j) / 2 is guaranteed to be ≥ i and < j. Using (i + j) / 2, therefore, seems like as good a choice as any for correctness's sake, and leads to an efficient solution as well: binary search.

We give a Java implementation of this number-guessing game in Listing 4.5. The guesses are stored in a list to be printed out once the loop terminates, so we have a record of how the number was guessed. Note that mid may never actually equal value, requiring the additional membership test after the loop to ensure that the final guess — the correct answer — is output.

Exercise 4.9 Give an example where mid does not ever equal value.

Exercise 4.10 Inside the loop, is it ever possible to guess the same number twice? Why or why not.

Listing 4.5: Guessing Numbers

```java
import java.util.*;
class binary1
{

    static void guess (int value)
    {
        //Requires: value is in [1..100]
        //Effects: outputs sequence of choices to guess the number
        int i = 1, j = 100, mid = 0;
        List<Integer> guesses = new LinkedList<Integer>();
        while (!(i == j))
        {
            //Invariant: value is in [i..j]; i <= j
            //Variant: j - i
            mid = (i + j) / 2;
            guesses.add (mid);
            if (mid == value)
                i = j = mid;
            else if (mid < value)
                i = mid + 1;
```

```
       else
          j = mid − 1;
    }
    if (!guesses.contains (i)) guesses.add (i);
    System.out.println (guesses);
  }

  public static void main (String[] args)
  {
    guess (83);
  }
}
```

4.2.2   Binary Search in General

Given a sorted array where no value is preceded by a larger one, we can perform a binary search to determine whether an element exists in the array or not. If the element does exist, we would like to return its position in the array. The only difference in this case, as compared to when we were guessing numbers, is that the saught-after element may not exist in the array. Thus, an invariant that states that a value is guaranteed to be within some prescribed subarray is too strong to establish a postcondition claiming that we have found the element. This parallels the situation we came across in linear search, where we had to weaken the invariant in order to allow for the possibility that an item was not present.

There are several good ways of doing this. (There are even more bad ways of doing this — see 4.2.4.) The one we employ uses the following invariant: "a[0..i−1] < value; a[j..a.length−1] >= value". If we again terminate the loop when i and j are equal, then i is the first index that might equal value. If it does, we are done. If it doesn't, value does not exist in the array: it cannot exist to the left of i because all those elements are too small, and it cannot be to the right because a[i] was too big already.

To begin, we can set i = 0 and j = a.length. This might come as a surprise, but if we set j = a.length − 1 as might result from experience, we'd possibly invalidate the invariant before entering the loop. This is because the invariant would state that a[j] >= value, and we have no evidence this is true.

The Java implementation is in Listing 4.6. The structure is similar to the number-guessing game, though there is one important difference if we look at the **if** statement within the loop. Here, we only consider two cases, instead of three as in the number-guessing program. The reason is that we have incorporated the case where we have found the element into the second condition, where we update j accordingly. Evidently, then, we may find the element in mid, and continue iterating the loop just to bring the two indices together. While this may be true, causing extra comparisons in some cases, the current approach does simplify the correctness argument and results more naturally from the invariant.

Listing 4.6: Array Binary Search

```
class binary2
{

    static int search (int[] a, int value)
    {
    //Effects: returns location of value in a, or -1 if not present
        int i = 0, j = a.length, mid = 0;
        while (!(i == j))
        {
            //Invariant: a[0..i-1] < value; a[j..a.length-1] >= value;
            //0 <= i <= j <= a.length
            //Variant: j - i
            mid = (i + j) / 2;
            if (a[mid] < value)
                i = mid + 1;
            else
                j = mid;
        }
        //{a[0..i-1] < value; a[i..a.length] >= value}
        if ((i == a.length) || (a[i] != value))
            return (-1);
        else
            return (i);
    }

    public static void main (String[] args)
    {
        int[] a = {3, 3};
        System.out.println (search(a, 0));
        System.out.println (search(a, 12));
    }
}
```

Exercise 4.11   What if we set j = mid − 1 in the loop body here instead of j = mid? Is the invariant preserved? Does the variant decrease on each iteration? Are you feeling deja vu?

Exercise 4.12   What if the element we are searching for exists more than once in the array? Do we have problems?

By messing around with the number-guessing program or the general binary search, you'd be convinced that binary search is much faster than linear search. In particular, the number-guessing program takes no more than seven guesses to figure out the number between 1 and 100. Considering the worst-case scenario for linear-search is to make 100 guesses, we're doing OK.

So, how fast is binary search, really? Recall that we are usually interested in a runtime in terms of some input size n. In this case, we'd like to know how many times the loop executes for an input array of size n. To get an idea, after one iteration of binary search, we have narrowed down the possible search space to about $n/2$ elements. Among these $n/2$ elements, the next iteration eliminates half, so that we then have $n/4$ elements to deal with. This process continues, until we divide the search space into just one element and terminate. Of course, we might get lucky and find the required element on the first guess; but we are looking for the worst-case time here, so that we know that no execution can do worse. After i iterations, then, we have about $n/2^i$ elements remaining to search. When $n/2^i = 1$, we will terminate the loop; how long does it take for us to reach this case? Solving for i, we have $2^i = n$, or $i = log2n$. That is, in the worst-case, we will take time proportional to the base-2 log of the size of the input array. We can thus carve up an array of a million elements with about 20 guesses, or an array of a billion elements in about 30 guesses.

4.2.3   Oh no! Overflow!

Imagine you had an array containing 2 billion elements and you tried performing our binary search on it. We just reasoned that the algorithm is correct, so you'd probably feel misled if the algorithm broke on an array of this size.

You were misled. Even with our invariant that establishes the desired post-condition and variant that shows termination, we will receive an overflow when operating on an array of this size. The problem is the line that calculates the value of mid. For example, if i has value 1 billion, and j has value 2 billion, adding them overflows the maximum value of an integer (which is $2^{31} - 1$). This occurs prior to the division by 2, causing a runtime exception to occur. What happened? Did invariants let us down?

The discrepancy between what the invariant claims (correctness) and what actually happens (overflow) can be remedied if we consider an implicit assumption we have been making all along. Specifically, we have been assuming that operators like + are the everyday mathematical operators, not the ones implemented on a computer. On paper, when evaluating i + j, we always have an answer, no matter how big. (Too bad. Answering "overflow" on math tests would make life easier.) On a computer, as we know, this is not the case. Sometimes, when operands are too big, + does not do the same thing as the mathematical operator. In short, our invariant would suffice for correctness if our computer-implemented operators were the same as the mathematical ones.

What can be done? One approach would be to include overflow checks in our correctness arguments. We could show that each statement is guaranteed not to overflow, then use this knowledge to prove that each iteration really preserves the invariant. Of course, such a proof would break down precisely on the calculation of mid: we have no way to prove that the addition performed is within range of an integer. If we are not willing to change the calculation of mid, we could enforce as a precondition that the maximum size of the array is, say, 1 billion elements. Then, the maximum value of the addition is at most 2 billion; no overflow can occur.

In a practical sense, it is unclear whether we should focus on overflows when reasoning about our programs. Of course, ignoring it caused a theoretically incorrect binary search here. But this is rarely the case; is it worth convoluting every argument with lots of "this line does not overflow"? Sufficiently alerted by this example, perhaps we can take a middle ground: proceed as before, but recognize the warning signs of overflow and explicitly deal with those.

Exercise 4.13 Does your Java installation allow you to create an array of 2 billion elements? Try experimenting with commandline switches that allow you to increase the size of the heap. Based on your experiences, do you think this overflow is worth worrying about?

Exercise 4.14 Replace the calculation of mid with an equivalent formulation that does not overflow.

4.2.4 Binary Lurch

It is just too easy to unwittingly construct degenerate binary searches that, when prompted with specific data patterns, do not work. For example, we might be tempted to start with the number-guessing code and try to minimize the number of changes required to convert it into a general binary search. In particular, we might try to keep the invariant the same, except that we include the possibility that the element is not present. Consider, then, the code in Listing 4.7, which valiantly tries to do this.

Listing 4.7: Binary Lurch

```java
class binarybad
{

    static int search (int[] a, int value)
    {
        //Effects: returns location of value in a, or -1 if not present
        int i = 0, j = a.length − 1, mid = 0;
        while (!(i == j))
        {
            //Invariant: if present in the array, value is in a[i..j];
            //i <= j
            //Variant: j - i
            mid = (i + j) / 2;
            if (a[mid] == value)
                i = j = mid;
            else if (a[mid] < value)
                i = mid + 1;
            else
                j = mid − 1;
```

```
      }
      //{if present in the array, value is in a[i..i]}
      if (value == a[i])
        return (i);
      else
        return (−1);
    }

  public static void main (String[] args)
    {
      int[] a = {1, 1, 3, 3, 5};
      System.out.println (search(a, 0));
    }
}
```

If you run this example, it will loop indefinitely. This little program is particularly capricious, though, because it will only do this in special circumstances
— for example, when you are searching for an element smaller than all other
elements, and your array is of a certain size. Otherwise, it seems to "work". In
terms of invariants, though, it's not hard to see the problem. Imagine we are
searching a two-element array (or subarray) for an element that is smaller than
both elements. We know that i < j, and mid will get the value of i. At this
point, j gets the value mid − 1, making j < i true. This violates the part of the
invariant that states i <= j, and immediately tells us something is wrong.

4.2.5   What's Missing?

The idea of binary search is not to be taken lightly; it can be used to solve other
seemingly unrelated problems as well. Here's one such example, adapted from
an exercise posed in [3].

Assume you are recording the student numbers of those students who have
successfully handed in some assignment. As luck would have it, the student
numbers of your 25 students just happen to be $1, 2, \ldots, 25$. Each time you receive
a new mark, you add it to an array of student numbers. After seven students
come by, your array might look like {2, 8, 3, 9, 5, 6, 1}. After all submissions are
in, you look at your array and, oh no, it has less than 25 elements! Shamefully,
this means that at least one student did not submit their assignment. How can
we determine who one of the (failing) culprits is?

This type of problem appears any time we have a set of size n possible elements
that we expect to appear, but we only end up with at most $n − 1$ elements
recorded. There must surely be at least one missing: how can we record information about 25 students in at most 24 array locations? The key here is that
we do not require that the array is sorted. In the case of the student numbers,
a sorted array would allow us to test each successive array position to ensure
that it is one greater than the previous one. At some point, we will not meet

this criterion and will have found the missing student. Something smells like linear search.

Back to our unsorted students. We have 25 student numbers, and an array of, say, length 24, so we know that one student whose student number is in $[1..25]$ is missing. We want one iteration of our binary search loop to cut this range in half so that we might conclude that the missing student is, for example, in $[1..12]$.

Using the idea of taking the middle of our range again, we calculate $(1+25)/2 = 13$. We can now think of our array as being composed of two pieces: those students with student number from 1 to 13, and those students with student number 14 to 25. Comprising the whole array in combination, one of these subarrays must itself contain a missing element. If we knew which one it was, we could continue searching on that portion of the array, cutting our search space at least in half as any self-respecting binary search would do.

If the portion of the array containing student numbers from 1 to 13 has less than 13 elements, we know that this portion of the array must be missing one of these required 13 students. Why? The reasoning is the same as above: we require 13 students to fit in an array of at most 12 elements. In this case, we can continue searching for the missing student in this part of the array. On the other hand, if this portion of the array contains exactly 13 elements, it is not missing any student from 1 to 13. We can see this because, not allowing duplicates, the 13 elements containing student numbers between 1 and 13 must hold all of these students exactly once. Since the whole array missed a student, and the student is not among those with student numbers between 1 and 13, we know that the missing student has student number between 14 and 25. We can therefore take those array elements whose values are > 14 and < 25, and continue our search there, ignoring everything else.

One remaining issue is how to separate, on each iteration, the students whose numbers lie between 1 and 13 from those that lie between 14 and 25. The simplest idea is to create two auxiliary arrays that will respectively hold these elements once we traverse the relevant portion of the input array. During the traversal, we inspect each element and add it to the end of one of the two arrays, depending on whether or not it is ≤ 13. After this, we can compare the lengths of these subsidiary arrays to determine which has the missing student; this is the one that we further search on the next iteration.

The Java implementation in Listing 4.8 (abstracting away from our student number prelude) requires that an input array, as well as low and high indices, be passed. These indices indicate the lower and upper limit of the range of the array elements. (In the student number case, we would have low = 1 and high = 25.) Our precondition is that the array contains fewer elements than that contained in the closed interval between the supplied lower and upper limit.

Not surprisingly, the loop invariant will state that there is a missing value in the interval [low..high]. At loop termination, low will equal high, so we have narrowed

down the possibility of who is missing from the array to a single value, which
we can return as the function result.

The variant is high − low. From the invariant and the fact that the guard is
not true, we know that each iteration is associated with a positive value of this
variant. Is it true that the variant is decreased on each iteration? We know that
mid < high because it is calculated the same way as in the general binary search.
Therefore, if we set high = mid, we are guaranteed to decrease high − low; the
other case is similar.

Listing 4.8: Something Missing

```
class missing
{

    public static int miss (int[] a, int low, int high)
    {
        //Requires: a.length < high - low + 1;
        //all elements of a are in [low..high]
        //Definition: oldA is initial value of a
        int mid = 0;
        int[] first = new int[a.length];
        int[] second = new int[a.length];
        int firstSize = 0, secondSize = 0;
        while (! (low == high))
        {
            //Invariant: a is missing a value in [low..high];
            //a is a subset of oldA; 0 <= low <= high
            //Variant: high - low
            mid = (low + high) / 2;
            firstSize = 0; secondSize = 0;
            for (int i = 0; i < a.length; i++)
            {
                //Invariant: first[0..firstSize-1] contains values in a[0..i-1] that are <=
mid;
                //second[0..secondSize-1] contains the rest of a[0..i-1]
                //Variant: a.length - i
                if (a[i] <= mid)
                {
                    first[firstSize] = a[i];
                    firstSize++;
                }
                else
                {
                    second[secondSize] = a[i];
                    secondSize++;
                }
            }
            if (firstSize < (mid − low) + 1)
```

```
        {
            high = mid;
            int[] newArray = new int[firstSize];
            System.arraycopy (first, 0, newArray, 0, firstSize);
            a = newArray;
        }
        else
        {
            low = mid + 1;
            int[] newArray = new int[secondSize];
            System.arraycopy (second, 0, newArray, 0, secondSize);
            a = newArray;
        }
    }
    return (low);
}

public static void main (String[] args)
{
    int[] a ={8, 2, 4, 5, 1, 9, 13, 18, 3, 12};
    int low = 1;
    int high = 25;
    System.out.println (miss(a, low, high));
}
}
```

Exercise 4.15

- If we allow duplicates in the array, even if the first half of the array contains the required number of elements, it may be missing a value. Give a sample array which exhibits this.

- Explain why the algorithm as presented still works in this case. Specifically, show that if the first subarray contains the required number of elements, it may indeed be missing a value, but the other subarray must be missing a value as well.

Exercise 4.16   Can we use a.length as the variant instead of high − low?

4.3   Flag Sorting

Our goal for the rest of the chapter is to study various sorting algorithms, and how we can use invariants to reason about their construction and correctness. While we are typically interested in sorting arrays consisting of arbitrary values, we'll start by sorting arrays that consist of only two element values. Then, we move to the case where we have three possible element values. There are two reasons why first studying these restrictive sorting algorithms is advantageous. First, it gives us an introduction to the use of invariants in sorting algorithms; second, we'll see the method applied almost verbatim in a more complicated sorting algorithm later.

4.3.1   Two Values

We begin by sorting an array that we know contains only two element values, such as 0 and 1; for example, {0, 1, 1, 0, 0, 0}. In this context, sorting refers to rearranging the elements so that the 0's come first, followed by the 1's. The sorted version of the given example is thus {0, 0, 0, 0, 1, 1}. Note that we will be interested in sorting any array made up of any two elements, not necessarily 0 and 1. The technique then readily scales up to sorting an array so that those elements that meet *any* given property come first, followed by the elements that don't meet the property. In this specific case, we are sorting the array so that the first x elements meet the property "equal to 0" and the remaining $n - x$ elements (where n is the array's length) meet the property "not equal to 0".

A crucial aspect of sorting algorithms, including this one, is that we are not allowed to modify the number of times that each element exists in the array. If there are 4 elements equal to 0 in the original array, there must be exactly 4 once we perform the sort; if there are no 2's in the original array, there can be no 2's after we sort. This is usually made precise by saying that the bags formed from the original and sorted arrays must be equal. Abusing analogy, if we throw the elements from the original array into a bag, and throw the elements from the sorted array into another bag, the bags must contain the same contents. If we didn't require this, we could just replace the given array with all 0's and claim that we've sorted it. This is redolent of a point we made in Chapter 1, where we said that it would make no sense to modify the input array prior to performing a search on it.

If we're given array a as input, we might try to achieve a postcondition of "a *contains a big ol' bunch of 0's followed by a big ol' bunch of 1's*". If we restrict this in the usual way to an invariant, we would try to claim at each iteration, "a[0..i−1] *contains some 0's followed by some 1's*". If the "big ol' bunches" part didn't give it away, this postcondition and resulting invariant are unsatisfactory. Why?

Consider trying to extend the invariant to include the next element in the array. We know that a[0..i−1] is sorted correctly, and we want to claim the same for a[0..i]. If a[i] is a 1, we can get away with doing nothing: just incrementing i preserves the invariant, because we are appending one more 1 to the part of the array that follows the 0's. If a[i] is 0, though, then what? We know that this offending 0 has to be placed prior to any 1's in the array, or we violate the invariant. However, we don't know where in the array this split exists, and would have to search for it each time. Evidently, we can do better by remembering this split as part of the invariant.

To account for this, consider the postcondition "*all elements in* a[0..i−1] = 0; *all elements in* a[i..a.length−1] = 1". Generalizing to an invariant, we claim "*all elements in* a[0..i−1] = 0; *all elements in* a[i..j−1] = 1". That is, everything to the left of element i is a 0; everything from i to just before j is a 1; and everything from j onwards is what we still have to figure out. When j = a.length, we will have our postcondition. We can initially make the invariant true by assigning i and j to 0, so that both parts of the invariant claim nothing about which elements it knows are 0 or 1. Let's summarize the structure:

```
i = 0; j = 0;
while (j < a.length)
{
    //Invariant: All elements in a[0..i-1] = 0;
    //all elements in a[i..j-1] = 1;
    //0 <= i <= j <= a.length
    //Variant: a.length - j
    BODY
    j = j + 1;
}
```

As we noted while discussing the fated postcondition, if a[j] = 1, we do nothing: increasing j maintains the invariant. If we have a[j] = 0, then we must do something to the array prior to incrementing j.

What can we do? First, assume i < j. This means that a[i] is a 1, because we know that element i is in the nonempty range a[i..j−1]. If we swap elements at a[i] and a[j], we have a[j] holding a 1, and a[i] holding a 0. If we increment i by 1 to account for this, we can then increase j as we hoped.

Second, what if i and j are equal? The range a[i..j−1] is empty, so we do not know anything about a[i] from the invariant this time. We do know that a[j] is a 0, though, so if we increment i by 1 to keep up with j, we maintain that the range a[i..j−1] is empty again, thus stating no more than we knew before. Additionally, a[0..i−1] will still be all 0's as required, because i was moved over an element that we knew to be 0.

In the Java implementation of Listing 4.9, we make one simplification. When i = j, we know that a swap of a[i] and a[j] will have no effect. We therefore do not distinguish between the two cases i = j and i != j: in the former case, the swap is harmless; in the latter it is essential.

Listing 4.9: Sorting Two Elements

```
class sorttwo
{

    public static void swap(int[] a, int x, int y)
    {
        //Requires: x and y are within bounds of a
        //Effects: swap positions x and y in a
```

```
    int temp = a[x];
    a[x] = a[y];
    a[y] = temp;
}

public static void sortTwo (int[] a)
{
    //Requires: a consists of 0's and 1's
    //Effects: modifies a so it has the 0's followed by the 1's
    int i = 0, j = 0;
    while (j < a.length)
    {
        //Invariant: All elements in a[0..i-1] = 0;
        //all elements in a[i..j-1] = 1;
        //0 <= i <= j <= a.length
        //Variant: a.length - j
        if (a[j] == 0)
        {
            swap (a, i, j);
            i++;
        }
        j++;
    }
}

public static void main (String[] args)
{
    int[]a = {0, 1, 1, 0, 0, 0};
    sortTwo (a);
    for (int i = 0; i < a.length; i++)
        System.out.print (a[i] + " ");
    System.out.println ("");
}
}
```

4.3.2   Three Values

We now extend this solution to arrays consisting of three different element values: 0, 1 and 2. This problem was proposed by Dijkstra [7], as an example of deriving correct programs via invariants, as we're about to do. Dijkstra's formulation was called the Dutch Flag problem, as his array elements were the colors blue, white and red; the goal was to rearrange the elements so that the blue ones come first, then the white, then the red. While we're far less patriotic here, the algorithm is identical; the particular nature of the three elements is irrelevant.

With two array elements, we sliced our array into three pieces: the 0's, the 1's, and the unprocessed. Here, we split the array into a further piece to account for the presence of 2's; here is the resulting invariant:

```
//Invariant: All elements in a[0..i-1] = 0;
//all elements in a[i..j-1] = 1;
//all elements in a[j..k-1] = 2;
//0 <= i <= j <= k <= a.length
```

Notice the introduction of k, which terminates the section of 2's. This variable takes the place of j in the previous subsection, so that when k = a.length, we are done and can conclude that the whole array is correctly sorted. We might therefore claim a variant of a.length − k. (Or, we might not, but for now let's just go with it.)

There are three cases to consider on each iteration, corresponding with the three values of a[k]. If it is a 2, we have a situation analogous to the case where a[j] was a 1 in the two-value case. That is, we just increment k by 1, extending the sequence of 2's that begins at a[j]. If a[k] is a 1, we have the situation analogous to a[j] being a 0 in the two-value case.

The new and therefore interesting case, then, is when a[k] is 0. We want this element to follow any existing 0's in the array, so would like to place it at a[i] and increment i by 1. Falling into habit might result in code for this case first causing a swapping of a[i] and a[k], and then incrementing both i and k. This does not work!

The problem is that a[i] ends up in a[k], and we cannot guarantee that we have placed a 2 in a[k]. As long as we have processed some 1's, a[i] will be a 1, so we'll end up putting a 1 in a[k]. Then, when we increment k, we have violated the part of the invariant that states everything in a[j..k−1] has value 2. Notice that if we do *not* increment k (only incrementing i), we do not violate the invariant in this way. This invalidates our proposed variant, though, since a.length − k is not decremented in this case. We are still incrementing i, so incorporating i in the variant would let us make progress without necessarily incrementing k here.

Exercise 4.17   Proper variant, please?

Here's where we stand.

```
int i = 0, j = 0, k = 0;
while (k < a.length)
{
    //Invariant: All elements in a[0..i-1] = 0;
    //all elements in a[i..j-1] = 1;
    //all elements in a[j..k-1] = 2;
    //0 <= i <= j <= k <= a.length
    if (a[k] == 0)
    {
        swap (a, i, k);
        i++;
```

```
}
else if (a[k] == 1)
{
    swap (a, j, k);
    j++;
    k++;
}
else k++;
}
```

The first case is still problematic, though, if we consider that it may violate the range-checking portion of the invariant. For example, consider the first iteration acting on the two-element array {0, 2}. We start with i = 0, j = 0, and k = 0. Examining a[k], we find a 0, and so the first if-condition executes, resulting in a meaningless swap and an increment of i. Now, though, i > j, violating the part of the invariant that states i <= j. Why is this range violation important? Consider that, with overlapping variables, two pieces of the invariant may both claim something about a single array element. For example, we may claim that a[0] has value 0, but also value 1, assuming that the first two clauses of the invariant make a claim on this element. One of these clauses must then be violated, evidently because we let ranges of variables overlap.

The only way that i and j will cross like this is if they are equal prior to incrementing i. Prior to the increment, the range a[i..j−1] is empty, so we can safely keep it empty afterwards. That is, if we end up with i > j, we can increment j. Symmetrically, the same situation might arise between variables j and k, as we may increase j on an iteration without correspondingly increasing k. We cannot let j and k cross, so we must test for this and adjust k accordingly as well. The Java implementation is in 4.10, but be sure to consider the following exercises to investigate alternative solutions.

Listing 4.10: Sorting Three Elements

class sortthree
{

    public static void swap(**int**[] a, **int** x, **int** y)
      {
    //*Requires:* x *and* y *are within bounds of* a
    //*Effects: swap positions* x *and* y *in* a
    int temp = a[x];
    a[x] = a[y];
    a[y] = temp;
    }

    public static void sortThree (**int**[] a)
      {
    //*Requires: a consists of 0's, 1's and 2's*
    //*Effects: modifies a so it has the 0's, then the 1's, then the 2's*

```
int i = 0, j = 0, k = 0;
while (k < a.length)
{
    //Invariant: All elements in a[0..i−1] = 0;
    //all elements in a[i..j−1] = 1;
    //all elements in a[j..k−1] = 2;
    //0 <= i <= j <= k <= a.length
    //Variant ???
    if (a[k] == 0)
    {
        swap (a, i, k);
        i++;
        if (j < i) j++;
        if (k < j) k++;
    }
    else if (a[k] == 1)
    {
        swap (a, j, k);
        j++;
        k++;
    }
    else k++;
}
}

public static void main (String[] args)
{
    int[] a = {2, 1, 0};
    sortThree (a);
    for (int i = 0; i < a.length; i++)
        System.out.print (a[i] + " ");
    System.out.println ();
}
}
```

Exercise 4.18   Let's replace the statement that executes when a[k] = 0 with the following:

```
{
    a[k] = a[j];
    a[j] = a[i];
    a[i] = 0;
    i++; j++; k++;
}
```

What is the invariant and variant now? Prove this.

Exercise 4.19   The standard solution to this problem slices the input array into four segments, as we have done, but instead of the unknown elements being at the right end of the array, they are the third component. That is, we break the array into a sequence of 0's, then a sequence of 1's, then the unknown elements, then a sequence of 2's. Develop this alternate implementation. Does this invariant follow more or less obviously from the postcondition? Is it more or less efficient? Does it have any other advantages or disadvantages?

Exercise 4.20   Solve the problem for an array containing four element values: 0, 1, 2 and 3.

Exercise 4.21   In Section 4.2.5, we came up with an algorithm for finding a value that is missing from an array. We created two auxiliary arrays to split up the elements, and then used one of these as the array to search on the next iteration. Use a version of flag sorting to dispense with this waste of storage.

4.4   Selection Sort

On typical machines, integer variables have a range consisting of about 4 billion values. If we continued the trend from the last section and tried to use it to sort arbitrary integer arrays, we'd end up with a program the size of an encyclopedia. Here, instead, we analyze general sorting algorithms.

Generalizing from the previous section, the input to our sort routine is an integer array, and the output is a sorted array whose bag is equivalent to the input array. By sorted, we mean that if we take two elements from the array, i and j, with $i < j$, we have that the element at position i is $\leq$ the element at position j. At all times, we maintain the implicit invariant that the array we are sorting has the same bag as the input array.

If a is the input array, a simple loop invariant we can try to maintain is "a$[0..i-1]$ *is sorted*". Then, if we terminate the loop when i = a.length, the postcondition is exactly that the whole array is sorted. This invariant will be true of many algorithms that scan the array data from left to right. In order to make the algorithmic development more obvious, we can strengthen the invariant so that we have less choice for what to do in the loop body.

Consider maintaining the additional property that all values in a$[0..i-1]$ are at least as small as any other item in the array. Together with the above, we are claiming at each step that the first i elements are the i smallest elements in the array, and that they are sorted.

Before incrementing i, we can maintain the first invariant property (sortedness) by choosing any element to the right of i-1 that is at least as large as a$[i-1]$ and swapping it with what is currently at a$[i]$. Incrementing i would then result in the sequence a$[0..i-1]$ remaining sorted, but we wouldn't necessarily maintain the second invariant property, unless the chosen element had no smaller elements to its right. Therefore, instead of choosing any element from among a$[i..$a.length$-1]$, we should choose one so that it is the smallest among all those elements.

The plan so far is as follows.

```
i = 0;
while (i < a.length)
{
    //Invariant: 0 <= i <= a.length;
    //a[0..i-1] is sorted;
    //no other element is smaller than any element in a[0..i-1]
    min = index in a[i..a.length−1] with smallest value;
    swap (a, i, min);
}
```

If we can solve the problem of assigning min correctly, we would be done. This
will require an inner loop whose postcondition allows us to claim that min is
the index of the element that we should place next in our sorted portion of the
array.

Exercise 4.22   Is the value of min always uniquely determined?

Introducing a new variable j to scan the remainder of the array, the crucial
invariant of our inner loop is "min <= *all elements in* a[i..j−1]". If we terminate
this loop when j is a.length−1, min will be the index we require for our outer
loop to perform the swap and reestablish the outer loop invariant. Prior to
incrementing j, we have to check if a[j] < a[min]. If it is, then j is the smallest
index among the elements in a[i..j], so we set min to j and increment j. Otherwise,
min is still the correct index, so we increment j without doing anything. The
Java implementation is in Listing 4.11.

Listing 4.11: Selection Sort

```
class selsort
{

    public static void swap(int[] a, int x, int y)
    {
        //Requires: x and y are within bounds of a
        //Effects: swap positions x and y in a
        int temp = a[x];
        a[x] = a[y];
        a[y] = temp;
    }

    static void sort(int[] a)
    {
        // Effects: sorts a in increasing order
        int i = 0, min, j;
        while (i < a.length)
        {
            //Invariant: 0 <= i <= a.length;
            //a[0..i-1] is sorted;
            //no other element is smaller than any element in a[0..i-1]
```

```
    //Variant: a.length - i
    min = i;
    j = i;
    while (j < a.length)
    {
        //Invariant: a[min] is smallest element in a[i..j-1];
        //i <= j <= a.length; i <= min <= a.length
        //Variant: a.length - j
        if (a[j] < a[min]) min = j;
        j++;
    }
    //{a[min] is smallest element in a[i..a.length-1]}
    swap (a, i, min);
    i++;
  }
}

public static void main (String[] args)
{
  int[] a = {4, 9, 3, 2, 1, 11, 5, 6, 1, 3};
  sort (a);
  for (int i = 0; i < a.length; i++)
    System.out.print (a[i] + " ");
  System.out.println ();
}
}
```

Exercise 4.23   What if we execute the outer loop so that, upon termination, $i = $ a.length $- 1$? Can we still conclude the postcondition?

The pattern exhibited in this algorithm is one worth dwelling on. We specified a loop invariant that we wanted to maintain in order to conclude the postcondition, as usual. To maintain this invariant, though, we found it necessary to rely on an inner loop — specifically, its postcondition. This inner loop requires its own invariants so that its postcondition is indeed justified.

This is actually not the first time we have seen this. Think back to the array rotation example (Section 3.3.2), where we required the use of a reverse operation as part of the main development. There, we specified the reversal as a procedure, relying on the postcondition in the rotation algorithm where it is called. However, in the reverse procedure, we used invariants to help prove its correctness. We could have alternatively placed the reverse code inside the main loop, making it an inner loop as we did in this section. The only difference is the location of invariants — and a hiding or exposing of the fact that we are essentially using nested loops.

How efficient is selection sort? Given an array of length n, the algorithm performs one swap per iteration of the outer loop, so it executes n swaps in total. However, the inner loop makes $n - 1$ comparisons on its first execution, $n - 2$

comparisons on its second run, and so on, until it makes one comparison before terminating. Using the fact that $1 + 2 + \ldots + n = n(n+1)/2$, we see that the number of comparisons is proportional to n^2. We would thus say that this algorithm has a worst-case, quadratic running time.

4.5   Insertion Sort

Let's go back to the weak invariant that we shied away from in the previous section: the first i elements of the array are sorted. This time, let's augment it not by the property that the first i elements are the smallest i elements, but that they are exactly the elements that were previously occupying the first i positions in the array. That is, the bags of the original first i elements, and the current first i elements, are equal. When i gets to be a.length, we have the postcondition, so the invariant is again strong enough.

At each iteration, we want to extend the sorted sequence forward to include the next element in the array. Notice that we can't use the previous technique of finding the smallest element not yet considered. The reason is that the invariant now states nothing about the values of the first i elements. Consider the following array: {10, 11, 15, 2, 12}. If we have i having value 3, our invariant holds, since the first three elements are sorted. However, the next element, 2, is required to be placed at the beginning of the array, not after the sorted portion as per selection sort. The final element, 12, is required to be placed just prior to the 15.

We can characterize a proper location for the new element, x, by stating that it should be placed after all elements that are < x, or, alternatively, before the first element that is >= x. If we use a forward linear search for this, part of our guard would be that the current element is less than x, so after termination we have found an index that is >= x. The new element might be the biggest one, though, so we also have to be weary of going off the end of the sorted portion of the array, similar to the situation discussed in Section 4.1 on the Linear Search Theorem. Once we find this index, we want to insert x there. To do this, we have to shift the following elements forward one position to make room for x. This would require a second loop, beginning at the right end of the sorted subarray, shifting one element at a time forward, and moving left to stop at the place we want to store x.

Exercise 4.24   Implement this version of insertion sort. The main structure is an outer loop whose body contains two successive loops that perform the linear search and shift, respectively.

If we begin the linear search from the right end of the sorted portion of the array instead, we can condense these two steps into a single inner loop. The loop will find the highest index j whose element is <= x, and ensure that the following location in the array can be overwritten with x. We do this by storing element a[i] in x — the new element we want to put in sorted position — and then claiming that the array elements without element a[j+1] are the same as the original array without a[i]. When we then place x in the vacant position a[j+1], we maintain that the array bag is still the same, and can increment i because we have added one more element to the sorted portion. Of course, x may be the smallest element, in which case we want to insert it at index 0 (and not go off the left end of the array). The Java implementation is in Listing 4.12.

Listing 4.12: Insertion Sort

```
class inssort
{

    public static void swap(int[] a, int x, int y)
    {
        //Requires: x and y are within bounds of a
        //Effects: swap positions x and y in a
        int temp = a[x];
        a[x] = a[y];
        a[y] = temp;
    }

    static void sort(int[] a)
    {
        //Effects: sorts a in increasing order
        //Definitions: oldA = a
        int i = 0, x, j;
        while (i < a.length)
        {
            //Invariant: 0 <= i <= a.length;
            //a[0..i-1] is sorted;
            //bags a[0..i-1] and oldA[0..i-1] are equal;
            //Variant: a.length - i
            x = a[i];
            j = i - 1;
            while ((j >= 0) && (a[j] > x))
            {
                //Invariant: -1 <= j < i <= a.length; x = oldA[i];
                //a[j+2..i] are all > x;
                //a[0..i] - a[j+1] is sorted;
                //a[0..i] - a[j+1] is same bag as oldA[0..i-1];
                //a - a[j+1] is same bag as oldA - oldA[i]
                //Variant: a.length - j
                a[j+1] = a[j];
                j--;
            }
            a[j+1] = x;
            i++;
        }
    }
}
```

```
public static void main (String[] args)
{
   int[] a = {4, 9, 3, 2, 1, 11, 5, 6, 1, 3};
   sort (a);
   for (int i = 0; i < a.length; i++)
      System.out.print (a[i] + " ");
   System.out.println ();
}
}
```

Note the delicate interplay between the invariants of the outer and inner loop. Just prior to incrementing i, the outer loop invariant requires that a[0..i] is sorted. After the inner loop terminates, we know this is true except for the element at a[j+1]. If we store an element in a[j+1] that is in proper sorted order, then, we will have the whole subarray sorted. The negation of the guard of the inner loop indicates that x is a proper element to place here, since a[j] <= x will hold (or x is the smallest element), and all elements after a[j+1] will be > x.

The outer loop also requires that the first i elements are always a permutation of their original i elements. After termination of the inner loop, we know that the first i+1 elements in the array, minus the one at a[j+1], are a permutation of the first i elements in the original array. If we then place the original element held at index i in position j+1, we add the missing element, and can conclude that a[0..i] is just a permutation of the array's original elements.

Insertion sort, like selection sort, is a quadratic algorithm in the worst case. This time, both the number of comparisons and number of moves may be proportional to n^2. When the input array has already been sorted, insertion sort takes only time proportional to n, because the inner loop does a constant amount of work (one comparison) for each of the outer loop's n iterations.

4.6   Quicksort

There are several sorting algorithms that have faster than quadratic running times, and we'd be remiss not to discuss one here.

Consider the following method for sorting an array. We choose an array element called the pivot, and conceive of all other elements as being less than, or greater-than-or-equal to, the pivot. That is, we have an array with just two different types of elements. We already know how to sort such an array from the topic of flag sorting (Section 4.3). If we sort like this, we end up with an array consisting of some elements that are less than the pivot, followed by all other elements. We'll call these portions of the array "halves", even though the split might not even be close to equal. (For example, if we choose the pivot to be the largest element in the array, we will sort the array into a left part containing all elements except the pivot itself.)

We can now focus on the two halves of the array independently. We'll refer to the left half as l and the right as r. If we could successfully sort the left half and also successfully sort the right half, the full array would be sorted: we know that no element on the left "belongs" on the right-side or vice versa, because of our initial split. To sort the left half l, we can use the same pivot idea. That is, we choose a pivot from this subarray, partition it using the idea of flag sort, and create two new array halves which we must sort in order to finish with l. We can sort r in the same way and, indeed, any subarrays resulting from this partitioning idea can be dealt with like this. At some point, we will partition subarrays so small that they become single elements. These trivial subarrays are already sorted, providing us a way out of the algorithm.

This is a prototypical recursive algorithm: to solve the original problem, we make calls to the same procedure we are currently defining. When these calls terminate, our original problem has been solved.

The partitioning step of quicksort uses a loop, and we better know how to verify those by now. In fact, we have little to do there, as we'll effectively use the flag sort that we previously reasoned about. In order to prove a recursive procedure correct, we will proceed as follows. First, we will give a variant for the procedure. As with loops, the variant must always be positive; in this case, it must be positive on every recursive call that is made. Additionally, each recursive call we make must ensure that the new procedure activation has a smaller variant, by passing variables which imply this. As long as each procedure invocation takes finite time (proved via loop variants), procedure variants guarantee termination of the recursion. We must also give a postcondition (an *effects* clause) that the procedure is expected to satisfy whenever it is called. We first show that invocations of the procedure that do not cause recursion establish this postcondition. Then, when dealing with the calls that do recurse, we can use our knowledge that any recursive call we make must result in its proper postcondition being satisfied. This, again, is similar to the invariants we used in loops. There, we were able to assume that the invariant was true upon loop execution; here, we assume that recursive calls will perform properly and so can rely on their postconditions when they are part of other invocations.

Invoking a quicksort requires three parameters: the array to sort, and the lower and upper indices between whose range will be sorted. The initial call of quicksort will use 0 and a.length $- 1$ as the lower and upper bound, respectively, so that the whole array gets sorted. Recursive calls will use these indices to hone in on the subarrays to sort on each call.

The procedure to perform the partitioning, partition, is obtained with a few surface changes from our implementation of sorting an array with two values. The procedure now takes lower and upper bounds, indicating where to sort; it compares elements against the supplied pivot instead of comparing to 0; and it returns the first index that is at least as large as the pivot, instead of returning nothing.

The pivot can be any element of a between the supplied bounds l and u. Consider choosing a[u], and supplying this to partition to partition the array around this value and obtain return value i. Choosing our variant as the gap between the bounds, u − l, what are the recursive calls to quicksort we should make?

We might try calling quicksort recursively, first with bounds l and i, and then with bounds i + 1 and u. If both of these succeed, we have sorted both halves of the array and they combine to sort the whole. The problem is that our variant is not guaranteed to be decreased by this choice. Imagine that no values are less than the chosen pivot, so that i and l have the same values. Then, recursing with bounds i and l does not decrease the variant!

If we first swap a[i] and a[u], however, we can avoid this. This results in the pivot being located in its final position, since everything to its left is smaller, and everything to its right is at least as large. That is, the element where the pivot is has been sorted, so we have no reason to include it in further sorting calls. We can then recurse with bounds l and i−1, and then with bounds i + 1 and u. Now we are guaranteed that the variant decreases on each call as required. The Java implementation is in Listing 4.13.

Listing 4.13: Quicksort

```java
class quicksort
{

  public static void swap(int[] a, int x, int y)
  {
    //Requires: x and y are within bounds of a
    //Effects: swap positions x and y in a
    int temp = a[x];
    a[x] = a[y];
    a[y] = temp;
  }

  public static int partition (int[] a, int l, int u, int pivot)
  {
    //Effects: modifies a[l..u] so it contains elements < pivot
    //followed by those >= pivot
    //Returns first element that is >= pivot
    int i = l, j = l;
    while (j <= u)
    {
      //Invariant: All elements in a[l..i−1] < pivot;
      //all elements in a[i..j−1] >= pivot;
      //0 <= i <= j <= a.length
      //Variant: u − j
      if (a[j] < pivot)
      {
        swap (a, i, j);
        i++;
      }
```

```
      j++;
    }
    return i;
  }

  static void sort(int[] a, int l, int u)
  {
    //Requires: 0 <= l <= u < a.length
    //Effects: sorts a[l..u] in increasing order
    //Variant: u − l
    if (l < u)
    {
      int pivot = a[u];
      int i = partition (a, l, u − 1, pivot);
      swap (a, i, u);
      sort (a, l, i−1);
      sort (a, i + 1, u);
    }
  }

  public static void main (String[] args)
  {
    int[] a = {4, 9, 3, 2, 1, 11, 5, 6, 1, 3};
    sort (a, 0, a.length − 1);
    for (int i = 0; i < a.length; i++)
      System.out.print (a[i] + " ");
    System.out.println ();
  }
}
```

The efficiency of quicksort is almost totally dependent on the choice of pivot that we make. If we choose a terrible pivot each time (i.e. the largest or smallest element), one half of the array will be much larger than the other half, leading to deteriorated performance. In fact, in this worst-case, the algorithm is no better than selection or insertion sort. If we take the upper bound element of the subarray as the pivot, as in the pseudocode, this can happen when the array that we are asked to sort is already sorted. We first take time proportional to n to perform the first partition. When we recurse, we end up with subarrays of size $n − 1$ and 1. We then take $n − 1$ steps to perform the partition on the array of size $n − 1$, then take $n − 2$ steps to partition the next array of size $n − 2$, and so on.

On average, though, we don't expect this to happen. What we expect is that the pivot will divide the array into two halves that are close to being equal. Each time we recurse, then, we deal with two subarrays that are half the size of the original array. From the time complexity analysis of binary search (Section 4.2.2), we know that we have to divide the array a number of times proportional to the log of its size n, until we then approach a subarray consisting of one element. Here, though, we do work proportional to n in the partition step, prior to making this division and recursing. That is, we first do n work via the partition step, then make two recursive calls that also take n total time to do their respective partitions $(n/2 + n/2)$. Each of these recursive calls take $n/4 + n/4 = n/2$ time to partition their subarrays, so in total we again have n time spent on partitioning. We keep recursing like this ($logn$ times) until we reach subarrays of one element. The time complexity, in the average, is thus $n * logn$.

Exercise 4.25   How can we use the three-element flag sort as the quicksort partitioner? What are some advantages and disadvantages of doing this?

Exercise 4.26   Imagine the partition step always resulting in one subarray that is ten times as large as the other. Is the time complexity still proportional to $n * logn$, or do we degenerate back to time proportional to n^2?

Chapter 5

Dynamic Programming

In this chapter, we investigate the algorithm design technique known as Dynamic Programming. We'll see that we can use standard invariant-based techniques to come up with and reason about such algorithms, thus further extending the power of our methods to tackle these types of problems as well. We begin by devising an algorithm to solve a particular programming problem, much as we've been doing all along. Then, we'll explain why that development would be termed Dynamic Programming, and describe the general structure and components of the design strategy. This paves the way for the introduction of more examples, and a specialized Dynamic Programming technique called Segment Tables.

5.1 Segments of Zeros

Our goal is to solve the problem of finding the longest segment of zeros beginning from each position in an input array. The term segment is analogous to subarray; that is, it is a contiguous set of array elements. If the length of the input array is n, we want to return an output array also of length n. For arbitrary position i in the output array, its contents j represent that the longest segment starting at position i in the input array ends at position j in the input array.

Consider the following input array: $\{0, 0, 3, 5, 0, 0, 0\}$. Table 5.1 shows this input array and the corresponding output array. In index 0, the output array holds the index that ends the longest segment of zeros starting from index 0; the correct value is 1. In index 1, the output array holds the index that ends the longest segment of zeros starting from index 1. Again, 1 is correct, since the next element in the input array (at index 2) does not continue any sequence of zeros. We have used nil to represent those indices that do not begin with any sequence of zeros.

Exercise 5.1 What are the longest zero segments for array $\{1, 1, 1, 0, 1, 1, 1\}$? Array $\{0, 0, 0, 0\}$?

Table 5.1: Longest Zero Segments Example

Index	0	1	2	3	4	5	6
Input	0	0	3	5	0	0	0
Output	1	1	nil	nil	6	6	6

There are two distinguishing features of the present discussion, as compared to those in previous chapters. First, we are asked to return n results, not just a single result. For example, when we found the length of a longest plateau in Section 3.6, we returned information about the longest plateau of the entire array. We did not, by contrast, return the longest plateau beginning at each array element. Second, here we have our first exposure to a problem that cannot easily be solved by continuing to scan to the right, augmenting our invariant to take the next element into account.

Exercise 5.2   Solve the problem of finding the longest segment of zeros in a given array.

Referring to the input array as x and output array as y, the desired postcondition can be stated as "*for all* i *in* [0..n−1], x[i..y[i]] *is the longest segment of zeros in* x *beginning at index* i". This is just another way of saying that y[i] gives the ending index for the longest segment of zeros starting from position i. If we try to generalize this postcondition into an invariant in the standard way, we would have that the first i elements of y are correctly set, and would next want to extend this to correctly set y[i].

If x[i] is not a 0, we can set y[i] to a nil value (however we wish to represent this) and move on. This is because no segment of 0's can begin at this index, no matter what happens later. On the other hand, if x[i] is a 0, then what? We could set y[i] to i, which is correct for the time being. But, consider what happens on the next iteration, if it too is a 0. We ostensibly must update the value of i we used, since it should now be i+1. If a further 0 follows, we may have to update it yet again, and so on. In the worst-case, the whole array will be 0's, and each y[i] that was previously set correctly will have to be updated. Combine this with the fact that we require an inner loop to do this updating, and we've created quite the (unnecessary) mess.

Ideally, we would like to set elements of y correctly the first time and not have to look back. The only element of y that we immediately know how to set like this, however, is the last one. If x[n−1] is a 0, then y[n−1] gets n−1, otherwise it gets the nil value. Starting from here instead of at the beginning of the array, we can try moving left instead of right, so that when we reach the beginning we achieve the postcondition. The corresponding invariant is "*for all* j *in* [i+1..n−1], x[j..y[j]] *is the longest segment of zeros in* x *beginning at index* j".

Assume we are about to decrement j; we must establish the correct value of y[j] before we do this. If x[j] is not a 0, we set y[j] to the nil value, indicating that there is no segment of 0's beginning at this index. If x[j] is 0, but x[j+1] is not, then y[j] should be j: the longest segment of 0's is this single element.

Finally, we arrive at the case where x[j] and x[j+1] are both 0's. The value of y[j+1] gives the index that ends the longest segment of 0's beginning at index j+1; we know that its value is correct based on the invariant. The value of y[j+1] must also end the longest segment of 0's beginning at index j; y[j] should thus be given value y[j+1]. To see that this correctly sets y[j], imagine that there is actually a segment of 0's beginning at x[j] that ends after index y[j+1]. Then, we could use this proposed longer segment (without its first element) as the longest segment starting at index j+1. However, we know that we have already found the longest segment starting at index j+1, so this proposed longer segment of 0's cannot exist.

We thus have a means of filling in array y, starting from index n−1 and working our way towards index 0. Using a value of -1 to store nil, we present the Java implementation in Listing 5.1. We have incorporated the base case (where j points to the final element of x) into the loop, instead of dealing with it separately as per the discussion here. While it does add another if-condition to the loop body, it helps avoid dealing with the special case of an empty x array that would result if we tried to set y[x.length] correctly prior to loop entry.

Listing 5.1: Longest Zero Segments

```
class zeros
{

    static int[] zeroSegs (int[] x)
    {
        //Effects: returns ending indices of longest zero segments in x
        int j;
        int[] y = new int[x.length];
        j = x.length − 1;
        while (j >= 0)
        {
            //Invariant: y[j+1..x.length] are the indices ending longest segments
            //Variant: j
            if (x[j] != 0)
                y[j] = −1;
            else if ((x[j] == 0) && (j == x.length − 1))
                y[j] = j;
            else if ((x[j] == 0) && (x[j+1] != 0))
                y[j] = j;
            else
                y[j] = y[j+1];
            j = j − 1;
        }
        return (y);
    }

    public static void main (String[] args)
    {
```

```
int[] x = {0, 0, 3, 5, 0, 0, 0};
int[] y = zeroSegs (x);
for (int i = 0; i < x.length; i++)
    System.out.print (y[i] + " ");
System.out.println ("");
    }
}
```

5.2   What is Dynamic Programming?

In the previous section, to find the longest zero-segment starting at index i, we relied on the presence of the longest zero-segment beginning at index i+1. That is, we computed solutions to problems in such a way that, when we wanted to solve the problem for a new index, we had the solution to the required index already available. In general, we can think of the array we constructed as a table that we gradually filled in during program execution, and from which we retrieved solutions to previous problems in order to solve future ones. Of course, this array is not so much a table as a row or column of data, since after all it is just a one-dimensional array. We will see an example of a two-dimensional table of results in the next section. Regardless, the concept is the same: storing intermediate results to look them up later. This is the essence of Dynamic Programming.

Is this really something new? Consider, for example, the development in Section 3.7, where we found the segment with the largest sum. In trying to extend the invariant to cover the next element i, we found that storing information about the largest-sum segment ending at element i−1 was useful. In other words, we solved a different problem (largest sum-segment ending at a given index) and then "looked up" its result to help extend the solution to the main problem. Lacking the construction of a table, this would not be considered Dynamic Programming, but in terms of invariants, it is harder to make this distinction. When we solved the problem of longest zero-segments, the loop invariant made a claim on a portion of the output array we were constructing; in the segment-sum problem, it made claims on the single datum (end) that we were maintaining. The only difference is the amount of information stored by the invariant.

Notice that the zero-segment problem was cast in such a way as to make the creation of an output array inevitable. How else could we return information about each index of the input array? Often, though, the algorithm we are seeking will not explicitly require the creation of a column or table of data to be output. Instead, the information we store in such a table will be used during program execution, helping us look up solutions to subproblems in order to facilitate the main solution. For this reason, it is helpful to understand when we are algorithmically allowed to combine subproblems in this way to solve bigger problems; and why we store this information instead of computing it when really necessary.

In the zero-segment problem, why could we use the solution to the longest segment starting at index i+1 to ascertain the longest segment beginning at index i? The reason is that the algorithm exhibits optimal substructure [5]. That is, solutions to bigger problems are constructed from solutions to a number of subproblems — in this case, just one subproblem. Convincing oneself that this is indeed true is usually achieved using a contradiction argument. Assume we have created an optimal solution to a problem using solutions to subproblems. We should have constructed a loop invariant that claims that the solutions to these subproblems are correct. Then, we show that if the problem has a better or more optimal solution than the one we found, it could be used to create a better solution to one of the subproblems that we already know is optimal, giving us a contradiction.

Why should we take advantage of such optimal substructure? Consider again the zero-segments example, but this time let's try to solve it without looking up any previously-obtained information. Beginning at each array index, we can scan to the right until we find an element that is not a 0. This surely gives us all the longest zero-segments, whose lengths we can store as required. The problem, though, is that we have produced an algorithm that takes time proportional to n^2, where n is the length of the input array. The previous Dynamic Programming version took time only linear in n. While this in itself is substantial, there are situations (one of which follows in the next section) where a Dynamic Program may lead to a polynomial-time algorithm when a "brute-force" version is exponential. The speedup that results from looking up solutions to subproblems is contingent on the subproblem solutions being used multiple times throughout algorithm execution. Since we have stored their solutions the first time, whenever a less sophisticated algorithm would recompute them, we simply look them up. If we store solutions to subproblems, never to look at them again, we are just wasting storage.

As a case in point, imagine that in the zero-segment example, we recognize the optimal substructure of the problem and use solutions to smaller instances of the problem to build up solutions to larger instances. That is, to find the ending index of the longest string of zeros beginning at index i, we may use the longest segment of zeros beginning at index i+1. Instead of storing the ending index of the longest segment starting at index i+1, however, we opt to recompute it each time. We might then produce code similar to Listing 5.2. The endIndex procedure finds the ending index of the longest zero-segment beginning at the supplied index i. It includes a similar case analysis to what we saw in the Dynamic Programming version, except that it makes a recursive call to compute the longest segment starting at index i+1 instead of looking it up.

Listing 5.2: Slooooow Longest Zero Segments

```
class zeros2
{

    static int endIndex (int[] a, int i)
    {
```

```
    if (i == a.length)
       return (−1);
    else if (a[i] != 0)
       return (−1);
    else if ((a[i] == 0) && ((i == a.length − 1) || (a[i+1] != 0)))
       return (i);
    else
       return (endIndex (a, i+1));
}

static int[] zeroSegs (int[] x)
{
    //Effects: returns ending indices of longest zero segments in x
    int[] y = new int[x.length];
    for (int j = 0; j < x.length; j++)
       y[j] = endIndex (x, j);
    return (y);
}

public static void main (String[] args)
{
    int[] x = {0, 0, 3, 5, 0, 0, 0};
    int[] y = zeroSegs (x);
    for (int i = 0; i < x.length; i++)
       System.out.print (y[i] + " ");
    System.out.println ("");
}
}
```

Assume the input array has five elements. We first make a call to endIndex and ask for the ending index of the longest zero-segment starting at the first element. If the first element's value is a 0, we will make a recursive call that asks for the ending index of the longest zero-segment beginning at the second element. If this element too is a 0, we will make another recursive call, and so on, until we reach a non-zero element or the end of the array. In the worst case, the whole array will be 0's and we will compute the ending index of the longest zero-segment for all five elements in the array. This is all necessary to fill in the first element of the output array. The next call of endIndex will determine the longest zero-segment beginning at the second element of the input array. This may, again, cause recursive calls asking about the longest segments beginning at the third, fourth and fifth elements. We are duplicating work that we did on the procedure's first invocation — recomputing required information instead of looking it up. We have here another algorithm that takes time proportional to n^2.

To be sure, there are many algorithms where storing solutions to subproblems does not help at all. Consider a linear search algorithm that finds the first occurrence of a target element. We can conceive of this process of solving

Table 5.2: Sample Checkerboard

2	2	1	1
3	12	1	5
0	0	5	9
8	0	5	4

successively larger subproblems that make claims on larger and larger portions of the array. Why don't we create an array that tells us whether or not the target element exists in the first i elements of the input array? Simply because this information is unnecessary in solving the original problem. While linear search evidently exhibits optimal substructure, we cannot use this information to speed up the algorithm.

In summary, Dynamic Programming often applies when an algorithm exhibits two properties. First, we want optimal substructure: solutions to bigger problems are constructed using solutions to smaller ones. Second, we want that the stored solutions to subproblems are indeed used again in constructing solutions to other, bigger problems. If the first property does not apply, we will have trouble using the stored solutions in any meaningful way; if we do not have the second property, we won't look at them at all.

5.3   Money March

As an example of constructing a two-dimensional array of stored results, consider this problem (adapted from [5]). You are given an n by n checkerboard, where each of its squares is associated with a positive amount of money. Starting somewhere on the bottom row, the game involves moving a checker to somewhere on the top row. At each step, there are a maximum of three allowable moves. First, you may move the checker up to the square above. Second, you may move the checker to the square above and to the left, but only when the checker is not already positioned on the first column. Third, you may move the checker to the square above and to the right, but only when the checker is not positioned on the last column. For each square the checker occupies during the game, you receive that square's money value. Maximize the amount of money you receive.

For example, consider playing the game on the 4 by 4 checkerboard in Table 5.2. We are allowed to begin anywhere on the bottom row, so let's try beginning at the bottom left. We receive 8 units of money for starting here. Our two allowable moves are to move up (receiving 0 money) or to move up and to the right (also receiving 0 money). Let's choose the latter option. We now have three moves: moving to the square above (12 money), above and to the left (3 money) or above and to the right (1 money). It is hard to resist moving up; let's do this, giving us a total of 20 money. At this point, we can move up to the top row, grab two more of these money things and finish with 22.

The postcondition of our algorithm is "m *is the maximum money we can receive by beginning at the bottom row and ending at the top row*". What we cannot do is directly generalize this postcondition to an invariant: "m *is the maximum money we can receive by beginning at the bottom row and ending at row* i, *following the allowable game moves*". Why not?

Denote the bottom row as row n−1, the next row up as n−2, and so on, until the top row is row 0. We can make the proposed invariant true prior to loop entry by setting i to n−1 and m to the maximum amount of money found on the bottom row of the checkerboard (the lower left square in Table 5.2). Now, with the invariant true, how can we extend the invariant to include the row above? We might think that making the move that gives us the most money would maintain the invariant, but this is not true. In Table 5.2, both allowable moves result in a total of $8 + 0 = 8$ units of money, and apparently this is the most we can achieve from the bottom two rows. However, if we began at the lower right instead of the lower left, we could get $4 + 9 = 13$ units of money. Thus, our invariant is not maintained. Moreover, choosing the bottom-left square as the starting point evidently gives us no way whatsoever to extend the invariant to two rows, since we should have begun somewhere else.

Since we can't determine the single path from the bottom row to the top row that maximizes profit, an alternative idea is to determine the maximum money we can make by ending at each square. If we had this information for all squares on the checkerboard, the maximum money we can make overall would be the maximum money of any square in the top row. Thus, we are creating an array y, whose dimensions are the same as those of the checkerboard, and where y[a,b] is the maximum money we can gain by beginning anywhere on the bottom row and ending at row a, column b.

The specific elements of y that we can characterize in an invariant depend on the information necessary to compute further elements. To begin, we can calculate the elements in the bottom row of y by simply copying the dollar values associated with those squares. That is, the maximum money we can make by beginning at the bottom row and ending at a specific element on the bottom row results from beginning at that element. There is no other way to reach a square on the bottom row.

To calculate other elements of y, we can rely on the optimal substructure of the algorithm. We know that to reach the square on row a, column b (denoted as square [a, b]), we must have come from one of at most three other squares: the one below, the one below and to the left, or the one below and to the right. We claim that the maximum money we can gain by arriving at [a, b] is the maximum money we can attain at one of these three other squares, plus the money gained by landing on [a, b]. We store this value in y[a][b].

Why must this be true? Suppose that the maximum money we can achieve in getting to [a, b] is more than what we store in y[a][b], and we can achieve this greater amount by coming from square [c, d]. Our algorithm would thus have come from [c, d] as well. Subtracting the money we earned by landing on [a, b] gives us an amount of money that is greater than the amount we earned by reaching [c, d]. If y[c][d] were set correctly beforehand, we would therefore have a contradiction. We would know, by the invariant, that y[c][d] was correct, but under the assumption that y[a][b] was wrong, we have a bigger value for y[c][d]. We conclude that y[a][b] is correct.

To calculate an element of y, then, we require that the elements below, below and to the left, and below and to the right are already calculated. If we fill out y row by row, starting from the bottom, we maintain this condition. Specifically, when filling out row i, we have all elements in row i+1 already available. Each column in row i can be calculated by adding the amount of money associated with its square to the maximum money achieved through a legal move to this square.

The resulting Java implementation is in Listing 5.3. Method maxMoney returns an integer corresponding to the maximum money we can attain by playing the checkerboard game. The two-dimensional array x gives, for each square on the checkerboard, the amount of money earned for landing there. The two-dimensional array y will eventually contain, for each square, the maximum money we can attain by starting from the bottom row and moving to this square. We fill table y from the bottom, row by row, until all n rows are complete. Note that the bottom row is row n−1, and the top row is row 0. We then use one final loop to examine the top row of y and pick out its maximum value; this is what we return.

The first invariant in the code is "y[n−1][0..i−1] *are maximum attainable money*". Since the first subscript is fixed at n−1, we are referring only to elements in row n−1 (the bottom row). The second subscript varries between 0 and i−1; together, the two subscripts refer to elements 0 through i−1 of row n−1. This invariant (and others like it) is meant to convey that the specified elements have attained their proper values: they represent the maximum attainable money upon reaching these squares.

Listing 5.3: Money March Game

```
class money
{

  public static int maxMoney (int[][] x)
  {
    //Requires: all elements in x are positive money values
    //Effects: returns maximum money from moving up the checkerboard
    int i = 0, j = 0, n = x.length;
    int[][] y = new int[n][n];
    while (i < x.length)
    {
      //Invariant: y[n-1][0..i-1] are maximum attainable money
      //Variant: x.length - i
      y[n−1][i] = x[n−1][i];
      i++;
    }
```

```
    for (i = n − 2; i >= 0; i−−)
        //Invariant: all elements in rows y[n-1], ..., y[i+1] are maximum money
        //Variant: i
        for (j = 0; j < x.length; j++)
        {
            //Invariant: y[i][0..j-1] are maximum attainable money
            //Variant: x.length - j
            int option1 = 0, option2 = 0, option3 = 0;
            option1 = y[i+1][j] + x[i][j];
            if (j > 0) option2 = y[i+1][j−1] + x[i][j];
            if (j < x.length − 1) option3 = y[i+1][j+1] + x[i][j];
            y[i][j] = Math.max (option1, Math.max (option2, option3));
        }
    int max = y[0][0];
    for (j = 0; j < n; j++)
    //Invariant: max is maximum value in y[0][0..j-1]
    //Variant: x.length - j
    if (y[0][j] > max) max = y[0][j];
    return (max);
}

public static void main (String[] args)
{
    int[][] x =
    {{2, 2, 1, 1},
    {3, 12, 1, 5},
    {0, 0, 5, 9},
    {8, 0, 5, 4}};
    System.out.println (maxMoney(x));
}
}
```

Exercise 5.3   Modify the algorithm so it can deal with units of money that may be positive or negative. Argue that your new algorithm is correct.

Exercise 5.4   The formulation we presented gives a specific amount of money to each square, regardless of how the square is reached. Modify the algorithm so that the amount of money received for reaching a square is also contingent on the square from where the move was made. Argue correctness.

Exercise 5.5   Modify the algorithm so that it additionally takes a positive integer m as input. Each time more than m moves in the same direction are made, the amount of money currently earned should be halved. For example, imagine that m is 2, and we have just moved up twice (without going left or right). If we move straight up again, we will lose half of the money we currently have. If we move straight up one more time, we lose half of our money again. If we then move up and to the left, or up and to the right, we again have a fresh set of m moves before we are penalized again. Carefully give correctness arguments.

Exercise 5.6   When calculating row i of y, only row i+1 is required. In other words, all rows of y except the "current two" become unnecessary. Modify the algorithm so that y is only two rows, instead of n. What are the advantages and disadvantages of doing this?

Exercise 5.7   Imagine that we must begin at the lower-left square instead of anywhere along the bottom row on the checker board. Do we still require a Dynamic Programming solution? Implement and argue correctness for this version of the algorithm.

Let's briefly consider what happens if we recognize the optimal substructure of the algorithm but do not use a Dynamic Programming formulation. We might begin at a square on the top row, and recursively calculate the three subproblems corresponding to the ways in which we can reach this square. These three subproblems each divide into three more subproblems, giving us 9 subproblems beginning two rows below the top. If we do this n times, we will solve 3^n subproblems, and we must do this for each square on the top row. Thus, our quadratic Dynamic Program is well worth the effort.

5.3.1   Invariants and For-Loops

As exemplified by the Money March, Dynamic Programs often contain nested loops, each of which is controlled by a simple loop counter. We can of course use while loops in these instances, but it is often more succinct to use for-loops. For-loops collect the loop counter variable, the guard and the loop counter increment into a single statement, reducing the amount of code we write. Code that first initializes a loop counter, then enters a while loop whose last statement increments the loop counter is represented by the following template:

```
e = init;
while (guard)
{
   ... statement
   increment e;
   }
```

It is equivalent to a for-loop of the following form:

```
for (e = init; guard; increment e)
   ...statement
```

Since for-loops and while-loops are equivalent in this way, reasoning about invariants and variants with for-loops poses no new problem. To show that a property is invariant, we show it holds after the initialization of the loop counter variable and before loop execution. We argue that the loop body maintains the invariant as we have always done, taking care to include the increment of the loop variable. This same loop body must decrease the variant and each execution of the loop must coincide with a positive variant. The only difference is in the syntactic form of the loop.

Exercise 5.8   Rewrite the first loop in Listing 5.3 to use a for-loop. Then, argue that the invariant and variant meet their respective properties.

5.3.2   Recovering the Path

What if we are interested in the sequence of moves that results in the maximum attainable money? Notice that we currently know how much money we can hope to get on the checkerboard, but not the moves to get this money. One way to solve this problem is to create two-dimensional array z, with the same dimensions as x or y. We store in z[a][b] the last direction that we moved — u for up, l for up and to the left, r for up and to the right — in order to achieve the maximum money from the bottom row to square [a,b]. Once y (and z) are completely filled, we can search the top row of y to find the square that we should end at to receive the most money. From here, we use z to backtrack down the checkerboard based on the directions we moved on the way up. At each step, we add a direction (u, l or r) to a string variable. Once we reach the bottom row, we have stored the reverse sequence of moves required to receive the most money; we have also found the position on the bottom row from which we started. We prepend this position to the reverse of the direction string, giving us a complete trace of our steps. This version of the method is in Listing 5.4.

Listing 5.4: Money March Game Steps

```
class money2
{

  public static String maxMoney (int[][] x)
  {
    //Requires: all elements in x are positive money values
    //Effects: returns steps for attaining max. money by moving up checkerboard
    int i = 0, j = 0, n = x.length;
    int[][] y = new int[n][n];
    char[][] z = new char[n][n];
    while (i < x.length)
    {
      //Invariant: y[n-1][0..i-1] are max. attainable money;
      //z[n-1][0..i-1] are last directions to get these maximums
      //Variant: x.length - i
      y[n−1][i] = x[n−1][i];
      z[n−1][i] = 's';
      i++;
    }

    for (i = n − 2; i >= 0; i−−)
      //Invariant: all elements in rows y[n-1], ..., y[i+1] are max. attainable money
      //corresponding elements in z are last directions to get these maximums
      //Variant: i
      for (j = 0; j < x.length; j++)
```

```
    {
        //Invariant: y[i][0..j-1] are max. attainable money;
        //corresponding elements in z are last directions to get these maximums
        //Variant: x.length - j
        int option1 = 0, option2 = 0, option3 = 0;
        option1 = y[i+1][j] + x[i][j];
        if (j > 0) option2 = y[i+1][j-1] + x[i][j];
        if (j < x.length - 1) option3 = y[i+1][j+1] + x[i][j];
        y[i][j] = Math.max (option1, Math.max (option2, option3));
        if (y[i][j] == option1) z[i][j] = 'u';
        else if ((j > 0) && (y[i][j] == option2)) z[i][j] = 'r';
        else z[i][j] = 'l';
    }
    int max = 0;
    for (j = 0; j < n; j++)
        //Invariant: y[0][max] is max. value in y[0][0..j-1]
        //Variant: x.length - j
        if (y[0][j] > y[0][max]) max = j;
    String s = "";
    j = max;
    for (i = 0; i <= n-1; i++)
    {
        //Invariant: s contains last i moves on path;
        //if i <= n-1, [i,j] is next move
        //Variant: x.length - i
        s += z[i][j];
        if (z[i][j] == 'l') j++;
        else if (z[i][j] == 'r') j--;
    }
    StringBuffer t = new StringBuffer(s);
    t.reverse ();
    s = "" + j + t;
    return (s);
}


public static void main (String[] args)
{
    int[][] x =
    {{2, 2, 1, 1},
    {3, 12, 1, 5},
    {0, 0, 5, 9},
    {8, 0, 5, 4}};
    System.out.println (maxMoney(x));
}
}
```

5.4   Longest Upsequence

A subsequence is formed from an array by deleting zero or more of its elements, keeping the remaining elements in their original order. For example, if we start with array {2, 4, 6, 8, 10}, one of its subsequences is {2, 4, 8, 10}, obtained by deleting the third element. Another subsequence is {2}, obtained by deleting all elements but the first. The empty subsequence is a subsequence of any array. Note the difference between a subsequence and a segment: they both consist of an array's elements, but a segment requires these elements be contiguous.

An upsequence is a subsequence in which each element is at least as big as the element to its left. For example, {2, 5, 7, 9} and {1, 1, 2, 3} are upsequences but {8, 6, 7, 9, 12} is not. The goal is to devise an algorithm for finding the length of the longest upsequence [8]. We assume that all input arrays consist of at least one element.

The postcondition of the algorithm is "l *is the length of the longest upsequence in* a". Introducing integer variable i, this generalizes to the invariant "l *is the length of the longest upsequence in* a[0..i−1]".

Since the given array is nonempty, we can assign 1 to both i and l to make the invariant true prior to loop execution. After all, the longest upsequence for any subarray of one element consists of that element and thus has a length of 1.

The manner in which we update l to maintain the invariant has similarities to how we updated p in Section 3.6. In particular, l can be increased by at most one on each iteration. Why? Imagine the invariant is true at some point in program execution, so l is the length of the longest upsequence in the first i array elements. Suppose the next iteration increases l by 2, so that there is an upsequence of length l+2 within the first i+1 elements, and whose last element is that stored in array index i. We could then remove this last element of this supposed upsequence, yielding an upsequence of length l+1 within the first i array elements. This contradicts that we know l to be the length of the longest upsequence in this part of the array. This shows that on some iterations, we will leave l alone; on others, we will increase it by one.

The fact that we are dealing with subsequences here, not segments, is made obvious when we think about maintaining the invariant prior to an increment of i. When finding a segment meeting a specific property, we would have new segments to consider that all end at the new element under consideration and include the next k elements to its left. In contrast, here we have new sequences that all end at the new element, but which may include any other elements to its left. Thus, our new element at position i may extend a subsequence ending at any previous array position, not only the i−1st.

Consider an array whose first five elements are {2, 6, 7, 3, 1}. The longest upsequence here is of length three, realized by the upsequence {2, 6, 7}. If the next element in the array is 9, note how we can use it to extend the longest upsequence to {2, 6, 7, 9}. The important conclusion is that we can extend an arbitrarily distant subsequence at any time.

Prior to incrementing i, we must increment l precisely when we can extend an upsequence of length l to an upsequence of length l+1. That is, if we have an upsequence of length l that ends with an element no larger than a[i], we have a new upsequence of length l+1. We form this new upsequence with the elements of the length-l upsequence followed by a[i]. Thus, it seems that a further invariant is necessary, maintaining that m as the minimal rightmost element of all upsequences of length l. We can assign a[0] to m prior to loop entry so that this new invariant conjunct is properly established. The loop body proves troublesome, however. Here is a first attempt:

```
while (i < n)
{
  if (a[i] >= m)
  {
    l++;
    m = a[i];
  }
  else
  {
    ...
  }
  i++;
}
```

Consider the **else** branch, corresponding to when the new element cannot be used to create a length-l+1 upsequence. (It cannot because it is smaller than any rightmost element of a length-l upsequence.) Could we not just leave l as is and just increment i to maintain the invariant?

To see that we cannot, consider an array that begins with elements {2, 6, 8, 15}. Its longest upsequence is of length 4, and the smallest rightmost element of any length-four upsequence (stored in m) is 15. If the next element to process is 10, we cannot make an upsequence of length 5. However, if we do not update m here, it will become out of sync with what is true and violate its part of the invariant. The element 10 gives us a way to form an upsequence of length 4 whose rightmost element is 10. If the element after 10 is 11, we see that we can form an upsequence of length 5. If we did not update m to 10 on the previous iteration, it would still be 15, and we would miss the fact that l should increase.

The role of the **else** branch, then, is to update m as required, so that it is still the smallest rightmost element of all upsequences of length l. For a[i] to form an upsequence of length l with a smaller rightmost element, it must extend an upsequence of length l−1 whose rightmost element is no larger than a[i]. We are in a similar position as when m was introduced. Specifically, it seems we require m' to hold the smallest rightmost element of all upsequences of length l−1. If a[i] < m', we store a[i] in m'. Otherwise, a[i] cannot be used to form an upsequence of length l−1 with a smaller rightmost element. But can it be used to form a new upsequence of length l−2 with a smaller rightmost element?

The pattern is that to update l, we need the smallest rightmost element of upsequences of length l; we stored this in m. To update m, we need the smallest rightmost element of upsequences of length l−1; we stored this in m'. To update m', we would need the smallest rightmost element of upsequences of length l−2; we would store this in m", and so on.

Since we must eventually maintain n pieces of information in this way, we will use an array srm (Smallest RightMost) instead of m, m', m" etc. The loop invariant on srm will state "*for all j in* [1..l], srm[j] *is the minimal rightmost element of all upsequences of length j in* a[0..i−1]".

We initialize l to 1 prior to loop entry, so we only have to set srm[1]. As this array element is doing the job formerly given to m, it likewise gets the value a[0]. Inside the loop, if a[i] >= srm[l], we have an upsequence of length l+1. We thus increment l and then assign a[i] to srm[l]. Now, srm[l] is correct, but what about the other l−1 elements of srm? That is, can we use the element we just stored in srm[l] as the last element in shorter upsequences?

We cannot; the rest of the elements of srm remain correct. This conclusion requires making the observation that each element in srm is at least as big as the element to its left. To see why, consider two successive elements in srm, a and b, and denote the index of a as i. If b < a, we could substitute b for a to form an upsequence of length i that has a smaller rightmost element than what we claimed in the invariant. Evidently we cannot use a[i] to update any other elements of srm, because they are all at least as small as a[i] already.

The other case to consider in the loop body is when a[i] < srm[l]. This corresponds to the case where we cannot use a[i] to form a length-l+1 upsequence, but we may have to update some elements in srm so they remain correct. Based on the discussion of m, m', etc. above, we would successively try to use a[i] as a smaller rightmost element for upsequences of length l, l−1, l−2 and so on. If we scan from right to left in srm and stop when we find an index j for which srm[j] <= a[i], then srm[j+1] can be updated to a[i]. This gives the new smallest rightmost element of upsequences of length j+1, and maintains srm in sorted order as required. We can use a linear search to find this element of srm to update. If we additionally updated any elements to the right of j+1, we would violate the sortedness of srm. If we updated any elements to the left of j+1, we would be replacing a rightmost element with a bigger one (violating the invariant on srm), or replacing an element with itself (doing nothing). We thus only update srm[j+1] to maintain the invariant prior to incrementing i.

The Java implementation is in 5.5. Note that the linear search includes a clause in its guard that prevents j from dropping below 0. This situation corresponds with a[i] being the smallest rightmost element of any upsequence, so we have a new smallest rightmost element of an upsequence of length 1.

Listing 5.5: Longest Upsequence

```
class upsequence
{

    static int lus (int[] a)
    {
        //Requires: a is nonempty
        //Effects: returns longest upsequence in a
        int[] srm = new int[a.length+1];
        int i = 1, l = 1, j;
        srm[1] = a[0];
        while (i < a.length)
        {
            //Invariant: l is the length of the longest upsequence in a[0..i-1];
            //for all j in [1..l], srm[j] is the minimal rightmost element of all
            //upsequences of length j in a[0..i-1]
            //Variant: a.length - i
            if (srm[l] <= a[i])
            {
                l = l + 1;
                srm[l] = a[i];
            }
            else
            {
                j = l - 1;
                while (j >= 0 && srm[j] > a[i])
                    //Invariant: srm[j+1..l] > a[i]
                    //Variant: j
                    j--;
                srm[j+1] = a[i];
            }
            i++;
        }
        return (l);
    }

    public static void main (String[] args)
    {
        int[] a = {2, 5, 6, 8, 3, 4, 6, 6, 6};
        System.out.println (lus(a));
    }
}
```

The outer loop runs n times, and each inner loop can run at most n times. We thus have an algorithm that takes time proportional to the square of n.

The structure of this algorithm differs from that seen in the previous sections of this chapter in two important ways. First, we filled in the array srm, but the solution to the main problem does not exist among its elements. Contrast this with the algorithm in Section 5.3, for example, where the table includes, in its top row, the overall solution. The srm array did help us update I, though, so storing this information still serves a similar purpose. Second, notice that we did not begin by exhibiting any optimal substructure properties of upsequences. Longest upsequences of shorter array segments are not stored, and hence are not used to build up longest upsequences in larger segments. We nevertheless arrived at a formulation that relies on looking up information from a table of data. The point is that our standard reasoning techniques can sometimes directly help determine when such a table is helpful, and how it is to be constructed and used.

5.5   Segment Tables

In Section 5.1, we solved a problem concerning segments in a sequence. There is a general Dynamic Programming method for dealing with such examples, developed in [10]. We describe the method and its applicability, then apply it to solve several more problems. This streamlined approach allows us to focus on the optimal substructure of a problem, hiding details of underlying invariants.

5.5.1   Description

A relation is a boolean-valued function that is true for some pairs of input values and false for all other pairs of input values. For example, consider the relation $Q(x, y)$ defined as $x+y = 8$. Q is true for some pairs of inputs. For example, $Q(4, 4)$ evaluates to $4+4 = 8$, which is true. On the other hand, $Q(2, 3)$ is false, because it evaluates to $2+3 = 8$. When a pair (x, y) makes a relation true, we say that (x, y) is in the relation.

Given array a, we can define a relation $P(i, j)$ that is true for some segments $a[i..j]$ and false for the remaining segments. In other words, P contains certain segments and does not contain others.

As an example, consider the array $\{-2, 2, 6, 3, 3, 8\}$ and the relation $P(i, j)$ defined to hold when segment $a[i..j]$ sums to exactly 6. Then, P contains pairs $(2, 2)$, $(0, 2)$ and $(3, 4)$. These are all and only the endpoints of segments that sum to 6. Here, the relation may include more than one segment beginning at a specific point. With array $\{2, 4, -1, 1\}$, we have both $(0, 1)$ and $(0, 3)$ in the relation. Hence, if we had to write an algorithm for detecting all segments adding to exactly 6, we would have to maintain a two-dimensional Boolean array seg2 of results, where $seg2[i, j]$ holds **true** exactly when (i, j) is in the relation P.

If we restrict ourselves to relations that include at most one segment beginning from each starting point, we can do better. Namely, we can use a one-dimensional array seg1, where $seg1[i]$ holds the unique j for which $P(i, j)$ holds.

Table 5.3: Next Smallest Numbers Example

Index	0	1	2	3	4	5	6
Input	3	6	8	5	2	4	4
Output	4	3	3	4	nil	nil	nil

Table 5.4: Shortest Balanced Segments Example

Index	0	1	2	3	4	5	6
Input	1	1	0	0	0	1	0
Output	3	2	nil	nil	5	6	nil

If there is no j for which P(i, j) holds, then we give seg1[i] some distinguishing nil value. Relations with this property are called right-end-unique.

Are there interesting right-end-unique relations? We have already seen one in Section 5.1. The relation consisting of pairs (i, j), where a[i..j] is the longest segment of zeros beginning from i, is right-end-unique.

Of course, there is only one index j that can end a longest or shortest segment of any property starting from i. There are, however, other types of right-end-unique relations as well; we give both flavors in the following examples.

- The relation consisting of pairs (i, j), where a[j] is the next number to the right of a[i] that is smaller than a[i]. There can be only one such index j; an example is in Table 5.3.

- The relation consisting of pairs (i, j), where a[i..j] is the shortest balanced segment starting from i. A balanced segment in this context is one with an equal number of 0's and 1's. We assume the input array has only 0's and 1's. An example is in Table 5.4.

- The relation consisting of pairs (i, j), where a[i..j] is the longest balanced segment starting from i. Using the same data as in Table 5.4, the corresponding longest balanced segment table is in Table 5.5.

- The relation consisting of pairs (i, j), where a[i..j] is the longest plateau starting from i.

- The relation consisting of pairs (i, j), where a[i..j] is the longest ascending segment beginning at i. An ascending segment is one in which each element is at least as large as the one to its left. An example is in Table 5.6. Note that a single element is an ascending segment, so we can never have nil in the table.

We can often use these relations to solve additional algorithmic problems. For example, consider the relation of longest balanced segments. By examining each (i, j) pair in the relation, we can determine the longest balanced segment of an entire array. Similarly, from the relation of longest ascending segments, we can

Table 5.5: Longest Balanced Segments Example

Index	0	1	2	3	4	5	6
Input	1	1	0	0	0	1	0
Output	5	2	nil	nil	5	6	nil

Table 5.6: Longest Ascending Segments Example

Index	0	1	2	3	4	5	6
Input	4	6	7	2	1	3	5
Output	2	2	2	3	6	6	6

find the longest increasing segment in an entire array. Evidently, right-end-unique relations encompass a number of algorithms, so all we have left is to efficiently construct their elements.

5.5.2 Linear-Time Construction

Recall that we will create array seg1 for relation P, where seg1[i] holds the j for which P(i, j) holds, or nil if this j does not exist. The simplest way to construct seg1 is as follows. We keep a counter i that takes on values 0 through n (the length of the input array). For each such i, we scan to the right with counter j, looking for the j for which P(i, j) holds. If we find one, we set seg1[i] to j; otherwise, we set seg1[i] to nil. Though straightforward, the problem with this approach is that it leads to algorithms quadratic in n. We may end up with the situation where j scans all the way to the end of the array on each iteration of i. We perform $1 + 2 + 3 + \ldots + n$ steps, which is proportional to n^2 steps.

Producing a linear-time algorithm is contingent on the specific properties of the relation we are dealing with. There are two classes of relations that lend themselves to such algorithms:

- Type-0. These relations have the property that, if we begin from the right end of seg1, we can compute each seg1[i] in a single step. Since we perform n of these steps, we have an algorithm that takes time proportional to n.

- Type-1. These relations have the property that the overall algorithm is linear, even though some individual computations of seg1[i] may be linear themselves. In other words, computing a specific seg1[i] may take n steps, but computing all seg1[i] is guaranteed to take no more than an amount of steps proportional to n. For example, if each seg1[i] took n steps to compute, we would arrive at an algorithm proportional to n^2. However, consider a situation where the first element of seg1 takes n time, the next takes $n/2$ time, the next $n/4$ time, the next $n/8$ time and so on. In general, the ith step takes $n/2^i$ time. The maximum number of steps here is 2n, as can be seen by adding up the terms in the series for arbitrarily large values of n. We defer the discussion of type-1 relations to the next section.

In Section 5.1, we implicitly saw our first type-0 relation. Let P contain pairs (i, j) so that a[i]..a[j] is the longest segment of zeros starting from i. We characterize the elements belonging to P as follows: P contains (i, j) when a[i] = 0 and {(a[i+1] ≠ 0 and j = i) or (a[i+1] = 0 and j = seg1[i+1])}. If this predicate is true for particular (i, j), it means that (i, j) is in the relation. We have a conjunction of two terms, and so all (i, j) in the relation satisfy them both. The first, a[i] = 0, says that we must have a[i] = 0 for any given i that is related to some j. This makes sense: there can be no longest segment of zeros beginning from an array location that does not hold zero. For the i's that satisfy this conjunct, the second conjunct gives the unique j that i is related to. It includes two possibilities. First, we have the case where a[j] does not hold zero. Here, the longest segment starting from a[i] ends at a[i], so (i, j) is in the relation if j = i. Second, a[j] does hold zero, so that the longest segment beginning at i ends where the longest segment starting at i+1 ends. This latter segment ends at seg1[i+1], and hence this is the value of j for which P(i, j) holds. The relation assumes the existence of a dummy value a[n], holding any value besides 0. This is so that if a[n−1] = 0, the relation correctly associates j = i to i.

This characterization explains the construction of the array x in Section 5.1. We know that when x[i] is not 0, there is no j for which P(i, j) holds. We thus give x[i] nil (−1) in this case. The other branches of the **if** correspond to when we know x[i] holds zero; the only difference being that we explicitly deal with x[n−1] instead of adding the fictitious element. As long as we construct seg1 from the right, so that seg1[i+1] is available when required by the relation P, we will construct seg1 correctly.

Exercise 5.9   Can we add a new "or clause" to the parenthesized part of our relation predicate to avoid the reliance on the fictitious nonzero element at the end of the array? If so, show how. If not, why not?

In Section 3.6, we solved the Longest Plateau problem with a linear-time algorithm that did not allocate any extra data. We can also solve it with a type-0 segment table, by constructing an array seg1 for the relation Q consisting of pairs (i, j), where the segment beginning at element i and ending at element j is the longest plateau from i. We characterize this relation as containing the pairs (i, j) so that the following holds: (a[i+1] ≠ a[i] and j = i) or (a[i+1] = a[i] and j = seg1[i+1]). We assume the existence of a[n] and a[n−1], which are unequal. The maximum seg1[i] − i + 1, calculated for each i in 0..a.length − 1, then gives the longest plateau in a. With this relation as a basis, we arrive at the solution given in Listing 5.6.

Listing 5.6: Longest Plateau Using Segments

```
class plateauseg
{

    static int lengthPlateau (int[] x)
    {
        //Effects: returns length of longest plateau in x
        int j, p = 0;
```

```
int[] y = new int[x.length];
j = x.length − 1;
while (j >= 0)
{
    //Build segment table y
    //Variant: j
    if (j == x.length − 1)
        y[j] = j;
    else if (x[j] != x[j+1])
        y[j] = j;
    else
        y[j] = y[j+1];
    j = j − 1;
}
j = 0;
while (j < y.length)
{
    //Invariant: p is length of longest plateau beginning at any element in x[0..j-1]
    //Variant: x.length - j
    if (y[j] − j + 1 > p) p = y[j] − j + 1;
    j++;
}
return (p);
}

public static void main (String[] args)
{
    int[] a = {1, 1, 1, 2, 3, 3};
    System.out.println (lengthPlateau (a));
}
}
```

As a third example of where a type-0 relation is useful, consider the problem of finding the longest ascending segment in an array. We will construct array seg1 for relation R that includes pairs (i, j) so that the segment beginning at i and ending at j is the longest ascending segment from i. We characterize this relation as containing pairs (i, j) for which the following is true: $(a[i+1] < a[i]$ and $j = i)$ or $(a[i+1] >= a[i]$ and $j = seg1[i+1])$. We assume the existence of $a[n] < a[n−1]$, so that the final element in the array begins and ends its own longest ascending segment.

5.5.3   Conclusions

It's interesting to compare the algorithms that we get by directly using invariants as in Chapter 3 to those obtained from segment tables. In Chapter 3, our Longest Plateau algorithm did not use any extra data, and only scanned the input array once. However, without the insight that a longer plateau can be found by simply comparing endpoints, we would have constructed an algorithm running in time proportional to n^2. In the previous subsection, we formed a solution that also runs with time linear in the size of the input array, but which requires space proportional to the size of the input array to store the segment table. Additionally, we scan the segment table after creating it — another step not present in our earlier formulation. The benefit of the segment table version is that all we must do is come up with a way of characterizing the elements of the corresponding relation. From there, it is a streamlined process to create an implementation. You might say we are sacrificing memory to sacrifice insight. The same pattern exhibits itself in the longest ascending subsequence problem. As Exercise A.4 kindly asks you to show, both segment tables and standard invariants can yield solutions. The difference is that the segment table version uses the auxiliary table; the other does not.

In the next section, we solve a problem requiring both type-0 and type-1 relations. Importantly, it is a problem not easily solved without segment tables. There are many other examples where the use of segment tables makes an otherwise obnoxious problem more manageable. The point is that even when there are other solutions, the ones produced by segment tables are often easy to create, understand, and get right.

5.6   Longest Balanced Segment

As mentioned in the previous section, a balanced segment is one that has the same number of 0's and 1's. The task is to find the longest such segment in an array. If we can find a right-end-unique relation that contains (i, j) for each longest balanced segment a[i..j], we can choose the longest among these to solve the problem.

How are longest balanced segments related? Recall the relations in the last section: there, we were able to specify the proper j for each i by relying on other members of the relation. For example, when finding longest segments of zeros, if an element i is 0, the longest segment beginning there is the one ending where the i+1st longest segment ended. We want something similar for longest balanced segments.

Let's start with this idea: if a[i] is 0, and a[i+1] is 1, then the longest balanced segment starting at i ends where the segment starting at i+2 ends. For example, consider array {0, 1, 1, 1, 0, 0, 1, 1, 1}. The longest segment beginning at index 2 ends at index 5, so the longest segment beginning at index 0 apparently ends at index 5 as well. While this ends up being correct, consider trying to find the longest segment starting from index 0 in {1, 0, 1, 1, 0, 0, 1, 1, 1}. We do not have a 0 followed by a 1 here, so cannot use our proposed rule. We might try to remedy this by adding a case to our rule to deal analogously with segments beginning with {1, 0} instead of {0, 1}. That would take care of the current case, again yielding index 5 as the end of our longest balanced segment.

But what if the array is instead {0, 0, 1, 1, 0, 0, 1, 1, 1}? If we take 5 as the ending index for the longest segment beginning at index 0 here, we don't have a balanced segment at all. This results because we appended an unbalanced segment ({0, 0}) to a balanced segment ({1, 1, 0, 0). This time, we can say the longest balanced segment is the one that ends the longest balanced segment starting at index 4 — in other words, it ends at index 7. Should we add a third case to our rule to cover our segment beginning with {0, 0, 1, 1}? We would then have to deal with all other combinations of length 4 as well, including other balanced beginnings like {1, 1, 0, 0}, and unbalanced ones like {1, 1, 1, 1}. I can keep you in this paragraph forever with this type of reasoning. The point is that we've missed the point. Though we have solved for specific cases, we need a general and simple rule that subsumes these.

The general observation is twofold. First, if there is no shortest balanced segment beginning from i, the longest balanced segment relation contains no pair (i, j). After all, if there were a longest segment from i, we can use this as a shortest balanced segment as well, contradicting our assumption that there was no shortest balanced segment.

Second, if there is a shortest balanced segment corresponding to the pair (i, k), the longest balanced segment from i is represented by the pair (i, j), where j is the endpoint of the longest balanced segment beginning at k+1. Why can there be no longer balanced segment? If there were, then it must also begin with the segment a[i..k], and extend past the end of segment a[k+1..j]. It would therefore give us a longer balanced segment beginning at k+1, contradicting the fact that the relation contains (k+1, j). If there is no (k+1, j), then the longest balanced segment from i is the shortest balanced segment from i, by a similar argument.

We can therefore describe P, the relation of longest balanced segments, via Q, the relation of shortest balanced segments. Let p be the segment table for P and q be the segment table for Q. Then, (i, j) is in P when the following holds: {p[q[i]+1] = nil and j = q[i]} or {p[q[i]+1] ≠ nil and j = p[q[i]+1]}. The first disjunct says that if the element following the shortest balanced segment from i begins no longest segment, the longest balanced segment from i is this shortest balanced segment. (We require the convention that p[nil] = nil here, in the event that there is no shortest segment q[i]). The second says that we can paste the shortest balanced segment from i to the longest balanced segment that follows it to get the longest balanced segment starting at i.

We necessarily must construct the segment table q before p; for the first time, we run into a type-1 relation. That is, there is no way to compute each q[i] in one step, like we have done for all other segment tables. The most naive way to compute q would be to scan to the right from each position in the underlying array, counting the number of zeros and ones we encounter and stopping once they are equal. This may require scanning most of the array on each iteration; it is an algorithm that takes time proportional to n^2 in the worst case. If we were to do this, we might as well compute p in the same way, since we already lost our linear algorithm.

We can do better as follows. Beginning from i, assume we have a 0 in a[i]. If the element to the right is a 1, we immediately have the shortest balanced segment of {0, 1}. Symmetrically, if the current element is a 1 and a 0 follows, we have the shortest balanced segment of {1, 0}. Otherwise, we have a 0 followed by another 0, or a 1 followed by another 1; let's take the first case first. Assume the shortest balanced segment starting at i+1 ends at k. Then, k+1 is the first potential ending index for the shortest balanced segment starting from i. Specifically, if a[k+1] is a 1, then a[i..k+1] is the shortest balanced segment starting from i. If a[k+1] is a 0, we move to the first element after the end of the segment starting from k+1 and so on, jumping over shortest segments until we find a 1 or reach a position that begins no shortest balanced segment (or get to the end of the array). The case where a[i] is a 1 is symmetric.

Why can't there be a shorter balanced segment than the one found by this method? To see why, we first argue that no shortest balanced segment can both begin and end with the same element (0 or 1). For example, the balanced segment {0, 0, 1, 1, 1, 0} cannot be a shortest balanced segment, because it begins and ends with 0. (The shortest balanced segment here is {0, 0, 1, 1}.) Assume for contradiction that there is a shortest balanced segment that begins and ends with 0; it is of the form {0, z, 0}. The elements in the middle (z) must include two more 1's than 0's, since the two 0's on the ends make the whole segment balanced. Also observe that at no time can z combine with the first 0 to make a balanced segment, for then we would have a shorter balanced segment than {0, z, 0}. Therefore, at no time can we have scanned a beginning portion of z and have the case where we have seen one more 1 than 0. However, we know that z has two more 1's than 0's, so at some time we must get to the situation where we have seen one more 1 than 0. As mentioned, this shows that a shorter balanced segment exists, contradicting the fact that {0, z, 0} is the shortest. The case for a segment of the form {1, z, 1} is symmetric.

Now, we can show that jumping over shortest segments cannot cause us to miss a shorter balanced segment than the one we find. imagine we find a shorter balanced segment than a[i..k+1] (found by making one jump over the shortest segment beginning from i+1). Since the elements at our proposed segment's endpoints are not both the same, the elements between these must be balanced. These elements could be used to form a shorter balanced segment from i+1 (that ends before k), contradicting the fact that we have computed the shortest balanced segment from i+1. We can extend this argument to any number of jumps: each one is guaranteed not to miss potentially shorter segments.

The Java implementation for computing the longest balanced segment is in Listing 5.7. We have divided the work into three functions. The first computes the shortest balanced segment table by testing possible candidates in j for the shortest balanced segment beginning at each i. The first candidate is j+1, corresponding to a length-2 segment. The loop terminates when the endpoints of the segment are equal, or when j reaches a point where there is no further shortest balanced segment. The second function uses this table to create the longest balanced segment table. The third function uses this latter table to compute the length of the longest balanced segment, by comparing the gap between all endpoints of the balanced segments.

Listing 5.7: Longest Balanced Segment

```
class longestbal
{

  static int[] sbs(int[] a)
  {
    //Effects: returns shortest balanced segment table
    int i, j;
    int[] q = new int[a.length];
    for (i = a.length − 1; i >= 0; i−−)
    {
      //Fill in shortest balanced segment table q
      j = i + 1;
      while (j < a.length && q[j] != −1 && a[i] == a[j])
        //Variant: a.length - j
        j = q[j] + 1;
      if (j < a.length && a[i] != a[j]) q[i] = j;
      else q[i] = −1;
    }
    return (q);
  }

  static int[] lbs(int[] a)
  {
    //Effects: returns longest balanced segment table
    int i;
    int[] q = sbs(a);
    int[] p = new int[a.length];
    for (i = a.length − 1; i >= 0; i−−)
    {
      //fill in longest segment table p
      //Invariant: q is shortest balanced segment table
      int s = q[i];
      if (q[i] == −1 || p[q[i]] == −1)
        p[i] = q[i];
      else p[i] = p[q[i]];
    }
    return (p);
  }

  static int lengthLbs(int[] a)
  {
    //Effects: returns length of longest balanced segment in a
    int j = 0, len = 0;
    int[] p = lbs(a);
    while (j < a.length)
    {
```

```
        //Invariant: p is longest balanced segment table;
        //len is length of longest balanced segment beginning at any element in a[0..j-
1]
        //Variant: a.length - j
        if (p[j] − j + 1 > len) len = p[j] − j + 1;
        j++;
      }
      return (len);
    }

  public static void main (String[] args)
  {
    int[] a = {0, 0, 0, 1, 1, 1, 0, 1};
    int[] b = lbs(a);
    for (int i = 0; i < b.length; i++)
      System.out.print (b[i] + " ");
    System.out.println ("");
    System.out.println (lengthLbs(a));
  }
}
```

5.6.1 Type-1 Relations

The reason that the shortest balanced segments relation is a type-1 relation can be traced back to the structure of the **while** loop used to compute its elements. In a general type-1 relation P with segment table p, we begin with a candidate index j that must be at least one index to the right of the current i index. We then test if a[i..j] belongs in the relation. If it does, we are done and can decrement i. If not, we use $p[j] + r$ as the next candidate, where r is an integer ≥ 0. For the specific case of finding shortest balanced segments, we had $r = 1$. We also require of a type-1 relation that when we are about to execute the loop again, we have the property that $p[p[j]+r] > p[j]+r$. That is, we guarantee that j increases on each iteration. This, too, is true of the shortest balanced segment relation, since each time, j jumps over a balanced segment (or the loop terminates).

We can intuitively see why this construction yields a linear-time algorithm. The naive approach would have the inner-loop (to find j) scan through each element after index i, and this is what causes the n^2 worst-case. By having j jump over segments instead, the inner loop does not take n steps. In fact, if on one iteration it takes several steps to compute p[i], then the next iteration will take just one step to jump to index p[i] — a great savings compared to a linear scan. For a practical demonstration of this, consult Table 5.7; there, we show time taken for a naive and segment-table version to work on the same arrays of various sizes. The data make a convincing argument that the segment table version is linear, as it almost invariably increases by 0.01 seconds for each 100000 element increase. The naive version doesn't fare so well.

Table 5.7: Comparison of Shortest Balanced Segment Computations

Array Size	Naive Time (s)	Segment Table Time (s)
100000	0.01	1.012
200000	0.02	1.832
300000	0.03	3.055
400000	0.04	6.76
500000	0.05	6.739
600000	0.06	10.264
700000	0.06	15.051
800000	0.071	17.094
900000	0.08	21.405

Chapter 6

Graphs and Data Structures

Graphs are a convenient data type that can be used to model a variety of problems. For example, we can use graphs to determine the minimum travel cost among a set of possible routes, the minimum cabling necessary to connect a network of computers, or course schedules that take prerequisite courses into account. In this chapter, we use invariants to reason about a graph algorithm, then discuss graphs in more general terms. In order to apply invariants to data types in general, it is helpful to introduce the notion of class invariant. Combining class and loop invariants, we proceed with several examples of specifying and giving implementations for data structures.

6.1 Celebrity Identity

Let's say you are at a really jiving party (maybe the same one as in Section 4.2.1), and you want to determine if there are any celebrities present. A celebrity is a person who everyone knows but who knows no one. The only questions you are allowed to ask are of the form, "Hey Person X, do you know Person Y?".

As example, consider a party with four people (A, B, C and D) and the following information about who they know:

- A knows C and D

- B knows D

- C knows D

- D knows no one

Person A is not a celebrity because he knows person C and person D (and he is not known by everyone else). B knows D so he, too, is not a celebrity. The celebrity here is D: he knows no one, and everyone knows him.

Assuming there are n people at the party, the task is to ask a number of questions proportional to n to discern if there is a celebrity and, if so, who it is. Before doing this, though, we need a way of representing the "X knows Y" information.

One approach would be to use an array of sets via a declaration like Set[] x. Each element x[i] would contain the set of people that person i knows. Finding out whether person i knows person j amounts to a membership test on the set x[i]. We would then require a means to perform this membership test in constant time (i.e. with a fixed number of comparisons). Instead, consider a two-dimensional array of booleans: **boolean**[][] x. Here, x[i][j] is **true** when person i knows person j.

Row i contains information about who person i knows, and column i contains information about the people that know i. With this representation, we can determine if person i is a celebrity by determining two things. First, for each j, we require x[i][j] = **false**; person i knows no one. Second, for each j, x[j][i] = **true**; everyone knows person i. Testing whether a given i is a celebrity in this way takes $2n$ comparisons; in the worst case, we will have to test all i and so we have an algorithm that makes $2n^2$ comparisons.

Recall Section 3.8, where at each point in execution, we had only one person in mind as a possible majority winner. We might try this in our current context as follows. We begin with person i as our celebrity candidate, and make comparisons until we find a person that i knows, invalidating him as a celebrity. If this never happens, i is our celebrity candidate, so all that is left is to check that everyone knows i. Unfortunately, this doesn't help, as the celebrity may be the last person we test, resulting in execution time proportional to n^2.

The opposite of this idea is to begin under the valid assumption that all n people are celebrity candidates, and to systematically remove people until only one is left. If each question we ask removes one person, it will take just $n-1$ questions to find our sole celebrity candidate. We would then ask another $n-1$ questions to determine whether he knows everyone else, and a final $n-1$ questions to determine whether everyone else knows him.

Exercise 6.1   Can there be two celebrities at a party? Why or why not?

Assume i and j are two celebrity candidates, and we ask "does i know j?". If i knows j, we have learned that i cannot be the celebrity, so we can remove him from contention. If i does not know j, we are still in business: we know that j cannot be the celebrity, so he can be removed from our celebrity candidates. In both cases, we remove one person, so after $n-1$ questions, we have one candidate in mind, as we hoped. Person i is then a celebrity if everyone knows him and he knows no one; otherwise he is not a celebrity, and we know there are none at the party.

Our implementation is in Listing 6.1. We assume that two-dimensional array x is passed, and that the people at the party are numbered from 0 to one less than the array's length. A stack cands is used to maintain the set of current celebrity candidates. We use its push method to first add all people to the stack, making the invariant of the following **while** loop true prior to execution. Each iteration then removes one element from s — the one that we know cannot be a celebrity based on the question asked. Once the loop terminates, we know that there is just one element left on the stack; this is the celebrity candidate.

Note that any data structure for storing the set of celebrity candidates would work. That is, the order imposed on the elements by the stack principle does not contribute to the algorithm's correctness. We could have used a set, queue, list or array. The stack data structure simply gives an easy way of obtaining two of its elements — by successively calling pop twice.

Listing 6.1: Finding Celebrities

```java
import java.util.*;
class celeb
{

  static int findCeleb (boolean[][] x)
  {
    //Requires: x[i][j] is true exactly when i knows j;
    //the nonempty set of people in x are named 0..x.length - 1; x[i][i] are true
    //Effects: returns celebrity number if there is one; −1 otherwise
    int i, j;
    boolean isCeleb;
    Stack<Integer> cands = new Stack<Integer>();
    for (i = 0; i < x.length; i++)
      cands.push (i);
    //{cands contains all candidates [0..x.length-1}
    while (cands.size() > 1)
    {
      //Invariant: if there is a celebrity, it is in cands;
      //1 <= cands.size() <= x.length
      //Variant: cands.size
      i = cands.pop();
      j = cands.pop();
      if (x[i][j]) cands.push (j);
      else cands.push (i);
    }
    //{cands.size() = 1}
    i = cands.pop();
    //{i is celebrity candidate}
    isCeleb = true;
    for (j = 0; j < x.length; j++)
      //Invariant: celeb is true if and only if x is known by all people in [0..j-
1]
      //and if x does not know any people in x[0..j-1] besides himself
      if (!x[j][i] || (x[i][j] && i != j)) isCeleb = false;
```

```
    if (isCeleb) return (i);
    else return (−1);
}

public static void main (String[] args)
{
    boolean[][] x =
    {{true, false, true, true},
     {false, true, false, true},
     {false, false, true, true},
     {false, false, false, true}};
    System.out.println (findCeleb(x));
}
}
```

There is another way to solve the problem that does not rely on a stack. Let us introduce two variables a and b. The loop invariant will state that the celebrity is in the union of b and the elements of a..n−1. Prior to loop entry, we set b to 0 and a to 1 to establish this invariant. When a = n under this invariant, the candidate set for the celebrity consists of n..n−1 (empty) and b, so the only possible celebrity is b. In the loop, we ask whether a knows b. If he does, a is not the celebrity and we want to remove him from the candidate set. We thus increment a. Otherwise, a does not know b so b is not the celebrity. How do we remove b from consideration? If we set b to a, we effectively discard b, but then we would be considering person a twice. Specifically, a is included in a..n−1 and is also b. Assuming our variant is (n − a) + b, it will not be decreased by this assignment. However, we can safely also increment a, since as we said person a is now represented by b. This reduces the variant and reestablishes the invariant as required.

Exercise 6.2   Give an implementation of this version of the algorithm. Be clear on your precondition and loop invariant.

Exercise 6.3   Which property on the numbering of people is required for this scheme, but can be handled when using the stack?

6.2   Graph Terminology

A graph is a data structure that contains a set E of edges, and a set V of vertices. Each edge in E begins at a source vertex and ends at a target vertex. With two vertices U and V, then, we may have edge (U, V) representing the edge beginning from U and ending at V, and/or edge (V, U) representing the edge beginning at V and ending at U. When we do not distinguish between the directions of edges, we have an undirected graph; otherwise we have a directed graph.

In Figure 6.1, we show a sample directed graph with seven vertices and eight edges. For example, there is an edge from vertex 0 to vertex 1, an edge from vertex 0 to vertex 2, and so on. Note that vertex 6 has no edges connecting it with the rest of the graph; nothing in the definition of a graph precludes this situation.

The power of graphs comes from interpreting the vertices and edges in various ways. For example, we might interpret the existence of an edge (u, v) as meaning that course u must be taken before course v. We might then try to find a sequence of courses that satisfy these constraints. Alternatively, we can interpret the vertices as locations, and edges (u, v) as signifying that there is a flight from city u to city v.

The celebrity algorithm from the last section can be cast into a graph-theoretic algorithm as follows. We interpret the vertices of the graph as the people, and edge (u, v) to mean that person u knows person v. In Figure 6.2, we give the example of people A, B, C and D that we used in the last section. Determining whether there is a celebrity amounts to finding a sink in the graph: a vertex to which all edges are directed, and which has no edges emanating from it.

The data structure we used in the previous section to represent the information about who knows whom is called an adjacency matrix. For a general graph, we can represent its information in a two-dimensional array a whose element a[u][v] is true when there is an edge between u and v. Our adjacency matrix in the previous section also had elements [i][i] set to true, so we implicitly have that a person knows himself.

The advantage of an adjacency matrix is that we can discern, in one array lookup, whether two vertices are connected by an edge. However, it takes time proportional to the number of vertices to find all edges emanating from a specified vertex. We did not require this information when finding celebrities, but if we did, an adjacency list representation would be more appropriate. Adjacency lists store a list (or set) of vertices for each vertex in the graph. This approach also saves memory when there are few edges; an adjacency matrix would still allocate a (mostly-unused) two-dimensional array.

6.3   Data Types and Class Invariants

Our two-dimensional array representation of graphs is slightly crude in the following way. When writing algorithms that use the graph array, we rely on the specific representation we have chosen. Imagine we write several algorithms using the array representation of graphs, and then we have a brainwave and decide to use an adjacency list representation instead. We'd have to rewrite all the algorithms, and all because we changed the underlying form of a graph. This is unfortunate, as in a more general sense we are still using graphs.

What we failed to do here is abstract away from the notion of a graph; we have coupled the properties of a graph with a particular implementation. Separating these concerns admits further benefits as well. For example, we could provide two or more implementations of the graph data type, then switch between them

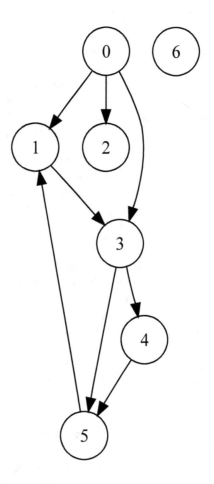

Figure 6.1: Sample Digraph

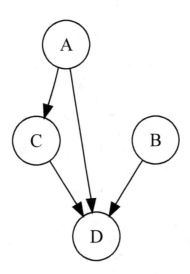

Figure 6.2: Sample Celebrity Graph

depending on requirements of different algorithms. Also, using only the specification of a data type allows us to focus more on its properties and less on an arbitrary internal structure. When reasoning about the celebrity algorithm, for example, it does not matter if a graph is represented as an adjacency matrix or adjacency lists or a linked list of edges. The reason why the algorithm is correct remains the same.

Two object-oriented concepts, inheritance and abstract classes, allow us to give a specification of a data type and later provide one or more implementations. The role of the abstract class, using specification variables, is to specify the operations and their precise meaning. Inheriting classes must provide implementations of these operations that are consistent with their abstract specifications. Specification variables will often take the form of mathematical objects such as sets, sequences, functions, or relations. Unfortunately, without formal definitions of these concepts, it is sometimes difficult to unambiguously state specifications. Abstract classes will also include an abstract invariant, that must hold on the specification variables. While abstract classes cannot be instantiated (so their objects can't actually exist), we consider their existence insofar as we want to ensure that the proposed invariant and operations are consistent. That is, under the proposed operations, the invariant holds, so that the specification is internally consistent. For example, imagine we are trying to specify a data type of sets containing at most 100 integers. This will be included in our abstract invariant, and would be violated if we were ever able to insert

101 or more elements into the set using the specifications of the operations.

Inheriting classes will be responsible for providing implementations of the data type operations specified in the abstract class. To do this, we use a *class invariant*. Class invariants are required to hold of all objects of the class once they have been created (i.e. after a constructor call) and in between method calls on the object. That is, we must show that object constructors validate the class invariant. Then, assuming the invariant holds, we must show that any method call coming from outside this object (that is within the method's precondition) reestablishes the invariant on its return. Compare this to the two conditions on a loop invariant. Variable assignments prior to loop entry can be likened to constructors, and loop iterations can be likened to code bodies (methods) that both assume and reestablish the invariant.

While class invariants impose relationships among the variables or restrictions on individual variables, they are also required to link their class' concrete state to the specification variables of its abstract class. This link allows us to show that implemented methods behave as expected by their abstract specifications. To show this correspondence of behavior, we imagine that every time a concrete method is called, the effect of its abstract counterpart also occurs, invisibly modifying the specification variables. We must then show that the class invariant still holds. It is important to keep in mind the dual purpose of class invariants: consistency of class variables, and linkage to the abstract specification. This will become clear as we investigate examples, beginning in the next section. The important lesson here is that we have a two-step process for verifying that a class correctly implements its specification. First, we show consistency of the specification; then, we show that implemented operations do what is requested by the specification.

6.4   Small Sets of Integers

Let's begin by providing two implementations for a data type of small sets of integers. We begin with a specification in Listing 6.2, telling us what exactly we are wanting to implement.

Listing 6.2: Small Set Specification

public abstract class smallSet
{

    //Specvar: set

    //Invariant: set *is a set of at most 100 integers*

    //Initialize: set *is the empty set*

    public abstract void insert (**int** e);
        //Requires: size of set *together with* e *does not exceed 100*

```
        //Effects: add e to set

    public abstract void remove (int e);
        //Effects: remove e from set

    public abstract boolean has (int e);
        //Effects: returns true if and only if e is in set

    public abstract int size ();
        //Effects: returns size of set
}
```

The specification includes, as comments, both the specification variable and invariant conditions. Here, the specification variable encapsulating our data type is set, and the invariant states that it is a set of integers with at most 100 elements. Following this is an initialize comment, giving the initial contents of set as an empty set. This empty set satisfies the invariant, since it includes no integers at all (out of a possible 100).

We continue with the specification of four operations that can be performed on our sets. The first can be used to insert an integer into the set, but only when the resultant set, including the new element, does not exceed 100 elements. The precondition here is necessary, since if it were unobserved, we could insert a new element into a set that already had 100 elements to violate the abstract invariant. Code that uses this data type must ensure that such preconditions are maintained prior to calling the associated method. In implementations, we can thus assume that the operations will be called only when the abstract preconditions hold. A subtlety here is that a call to insert with e already existing in the set is valid under the precondition, since the resultant set will have no more elements than before (and so no more than 100, as witnessed by the invariant).

The next two operations allow elements to be removed and tested for membership, respectively. Removing an element from a set cannot violate the invariant, and a query like has is also consistent by virtue of not modifying anything. The final operation allows the size of the set to be returned. In addition to being useful on its own, it is included so that calling code can verify, prior to invoking insert, whether the call is within the precondition.

We would now like to come up with an implementation of small sets that is consistent with this specification. As usual, the development is guided by invariants; here class invariants instead of loop invariants. One way to represent a set is as the elements of an array. For example, set {3,4,5} can be represented by an array whose first element is 3, second element is 4, and third element is 5. We also need a way to discern how much of the array corresponds to the set, since sets can be of different sizes. The class invariant we choose thus says that set (the specification variable) consists exactly of the first m elements of array a. We also state that m is the size of set. Consult Listing 6.3 for this invariant and the code for the remainder of our discussion.

Listing 6.3: Small Set Implementation

```java
public class smallSetImp extends smallSet
{

  //Invariant: set is elements a[0..m-1]; m is size of set

  int[] a;
  int m;

  public smallSetImp ()
  {
    a = new int[100];
    m = 0;
  }

  public boolean has (int e)
  {
    int i = 0;
    boolean found = false;
    while (i < m)
    {
      //Invariant: found is true if and only if e is in a[0..i-1]
      //Variant: m - i
      if (a[i] == e) found = true;
      i++;
    }
    if (found)
      return (true);
    else
      return (false);
  }

  public void insert (int e)
  {
    int i = 0;
    boolean found = false;
    while (i < m)
    {
      //Invariant: found is true if and only if e is in a[0..i-1]
      //Variant: m - i
      if (a[i] == e) found = true;
      i++;
    }
    if (!found)
    {
      a[m] = e;
      m++;
```

```
      }
   }

   public void remove (int e)
   {
      int i = 0, where = 0;
      boolean found = false;
      while (i < m)
      {
         //Invariant: found is true if and only if e is in a[0..i-1];
         //if found is true, a[where] = e
         //Variant: m - i
         if (a[i] == e)
         {
            found = true;
            where = i;
         }
         i++;
      }
      if (found)
      {
         a[where] = a[m−1];
         m−−;
      }
   }

   public int size ()
   {
      return (m);
   }
}
```

From Listing 6.2, the initialization of our implementation is required to correspond to an empty set. The way to do this is to set m to 0. The class invariant then claims that set consists of no elements at all from the array a, and that the size of set is 0. Both clauses are true; the first by virtue of the indices chosen from a corresponding to an empty range. Note that our constructor additionally assigns a new array to a so that we can successfully reference it later; we choose 100 elements since we know this is the most we can store.

Now, consider implementing the has operation. Abstractly, we know that has returns **true** exactly when e is in set. Since the first m elements of a are set, we want to return **true** exactly when e is among these elements. This is what the body of has does.

The insert implementation is more subtle. Recall that if e exists in the set, insert should do nothing. We thus begin by determining whether e is already present. If it is, the abstract set is unchanged by "adding" e again, so our set representation is unchanged as well. Otherwise, e does not exist, so must be added to our representation of a set. If we store the new element in a[m] and increment m to account for the new element, we again have that the first m elements of a correspond exactly to set after the operation (i.e. set with e included).

Continuing to remove, can we simply search through the array and remove the first occurrence of e that we find? (If we don't find e at all, the abstract remove will not modify set, so we can safely do nothing in this case.) What if e occurs more than once in a — can this happen and, if so, shouldn't we remove all such e values from the array? We can argue that only one copy of e can exist among the current array elements of interest as follows. From the class invariant, we know that collecting the first m elements of a form set. Also, m is the size of set. These two observations let us infer that each element of set exists exactly once in a[0..m−1] since there is no extra room to "waste" a space in a[0..m−1] for two or more copies. We are using m elements of a to represent m distinct values of set.

Listing 6.4: Small Set Test

```
public class smallSetTest
{

    public static void main (String[] args)
    {
        smallSet s = new smallSetImp ();
        s.insert (3);
        s.insert (6);
        s.insert (9);
        System.out.println (s.has (9));
        s.remove (9);
        System.out.println (s.has (9));
    }
}
```

For an example of using our small set data type, see Listing 6.4. We declare variable s as type smallSet, then dynamically bind it to an object of type smallSetImp. We use only the specification in smallSet, not relying on any properties of the chosen implementation. Note that this code satisfies the precondition of insert, since we are locally creating an empty set and then adding only two elements. If we wrote a procedure taking a smallSet parameter instead, we'd have to first test whether inserting an element would be allowable by the precondition or not. In the case that the set is already full and we are trying to insert a new element, we may raise an exception, return normally from the method, or whatever is appropriate. One inappropriate thing to do here, of course, is call insert and violate the precondition.

6.5   Another Small Set Implementation

There are many other ways to represent our small sets of integers. It is for this reason that the specification in the abstract class is important; without it, we'd have no way of verifying that two or more implementations can be used interchangeably. As an example of another implementation, consider Listing 6.5.

Listing 6.5: Another Small Set Implementation

```java
import java.util.*;
class smallSetImp2 extends smallSet
{

  //Invariant: set contains exactly the elements in v;
  //m is number of distinct elements in v

  Vector<Integer> v;
  int m;

  public smallSetImp2 ()
  {
    v = new Vector<Integer> ();
    m = 0;
  }

  public boolean has (int e)
  {
    return (v.contains (e));
  }

  public void insert (int e)
  {
    if (!v.contains (e)) m++;
    v.add (e);
  }

  public void remove (int e)
  {
    if (v.contains (e)) m--;
    while (v.contains (e))
      //Variant: copies of e in v
      v.remove (e);
  }

  public int size ()
  {
    return (m);
  }
}
```

Instead of an array, we use a vector. The class invariant this time relates the elements of the vector to the elements in set, but we cannot deduce from the invariant that the elements in the vector are unique. Therefore, when we want to insert an element, we do not have to check that it does not exist; we can just add it and create potential duplicates. Easing insert in this way causes a headache in remove, however, since now we don't know how many times e appears in the vector. Since we must remove them all, we remove successive copies of e until none remain.

6.6   Equivalence Relations

The specification of the data type we are implementing determines the operations that we are required to support. It is these operations that determine precisely what we should consider storing in the implementation, and what we can avoid storing. For example, imagine a set data type like the one in the previous section, except that we do not have the operations for determining membership or size. That is, we are removing the only operations that allow a user to query information about the state of objects of the type. Since implementations must be indistinguishable from the behavior in the specification, and we no longer have any way of making such distinctions, implementation is made significantly easier here. Specifically, a valid implementation of inserting or removing an element is to do nothing. We actually don't even need an invariant linking the implementation variables to the specification variables, because the user has no way to ask what is going on. For all the user knows, we are inserting and removing elements as requested; no one can refute this based on how the implementation works.

Of course, such sets would be all but useless. The point here is that we often don't need to store the information in the form that is expressed by the specification. We can often "forget" information, as long as we can still implement the operations as prescribed.

As a more realistic example, consider a collection of towns, initially with no roads between them. That is, starting at one town, we have no way to get to any other town. We are provided an operation connect that takes two towns and connects them with a bidirectional road. For example, let's start with five disconnected towns, labelled A through E. If we successively connect towns A and B, and B and C, we'd have the situation pictured in Figure 6.3.

In addition to connecting towns, we'd like to be able to determine whether there is a sequence of roads that we can take to travel between two towns. In Figure 6.3, for instance, we can move between towns A and C, but not between A and D.

When implementing this towns data type with these two operations (connecting and determining connectedness), we are not required to explicitly store all of the individual connections between towns. This is because we will never be asked to provide information about whether two towns are directly connected,

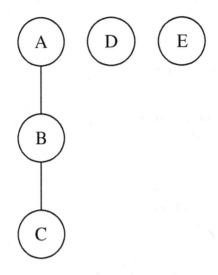

Figure 6.3: Sample Towns and Connections

or if they are indirectly connected through other towns. We must retain only enough information to determine whether two towns are connected in any way.

One way to do this is to imagine the set of towns as being split into a number of classes. Each town in a class is connected, directly or indirectly, to every other town in the class. We call the towns in a class equivalent. Additionally, classes contain all such towns; that is, classes are maximal with respect to equivalence. For example, again looking at Figure 6.3, we have three classes of equivalent towns: a class consisting of towns A, B and C; the class consisting only of town D; and the class consisting only of town E. A class containing only one town means that it is disconnected from all other towns, and a class with multiple towns means that each one is reachable from any other one in the class.

In an implementation based on equivalence classes, we begin with each town comprising its own class, since we begin with no connections between towns. When a connection is added between two towns, say A and B, it is clear that any town previously reachable from A is now reachable from B and vice versa. Thus, if A and B were previously not connected, we have a new class consisting of all towns previously in A's class and all towns previously in B's class.

The specification of the towns data type is in Listing 6.6, and an implementation based on equivalence classes is in Listing 6.7.

Listing 6.6: Towns Specification

public abstract class towns
{

  //Specvar: links

  //Invariant: links *is a set of connections between towns* 0..n

//Initialize: links *contains* (a, a) *for all chosen towns* a

public abstract void connect (**int** e, **int** f);
  //Effects: add connection (e, f) *to* links

public abstract boolean connected (**int** e, **int** f);
  //Effects: returns true *if and only if* e *is reachable from* f *in* links
}

Listing 6.7: Towns Implementation

public class townsImp **extends** towns
{

  //Invariant: towns x *and* y *are connected in* links *if and only if*
  *//*rep[x] = rep[y]; [0..t-1] *are the chosen towns*

  int[] rep;
  int t;

  public townsImp(**int** num)
  {
    t = num;
    rep = **new int**[t];
    for (**int** i = 0; i < t; i++)
      rep[i] = i;
  }

  public void connect (**int** e, **int** f)
  {
    int eRep = rep[e];
    int fRep = rep[f];
    for (**int** i = 0; i < t; i++)
      if (rep[i] == fRep) rep[i] = eRep;
  }

  public boolean connected (**int** e, **int** f)
  {
    return (rep[e] == rep[f]);
  }
}

Instead of fixing the specification to use at most a small set of integers (like in the previous section), we allow an arbitrary number of towns to be represented, starting at integer 0. After initialization, we expect that only the chosen towns will be used in future operations, and have not explicitly mentioned this in the operations' preconditions. The specification variable links is a set of pairs (not a set of integers as in the previous section). The pairs indicate the connections between towns. This means that, to add a connection from town E to F in connect, our abstract description is to take the union of links and the pair (e, f). The connected operation uses an intuitive description of what it means for two towns to be connected.

In the implementation, we use array rep (representative) to embody the idea of town classes. Each town t will be represented by town rep[t]. As the invariant states, two towns are connected in the specification exactly when they have the same representative. Upon initialization, we make this invariant true by giving each town t the representative t, since this corresponds exactly to each town being connected to itself. The connect operation must result in a state where each town previously reachable from e or f is now reachable from both, since these are the new connections admitted in the specification. To do this, we must give all towns connected to e, and all towns connected to f, the same representative. We do this by ascertaining the representatives of both e (in repE) and f (in repF), and changing all towns represented by repF to be represented by repE. The implementation of connected under our invariant is readily apparent. Since two towns are connected exactly when they have the same representative, and connected is supposed to return **true** when two towns are connected, we simply check whether they have the same representative. Consult Listing 6.8 for an example of using the towns specification and this implementation. As before, we do not rely on any properties of the implementation: we could replace townsImp with another valid implementation of towns and observe no behavior change in the tests.

Listing 6.8: Towns Test

```java
public class townsTest
{

    public static void main (String[] args)
    {
        towns t = new townsImp (5);
        t.connect (0, 1);
        t.connect (0, 2);
        System.out.println (t.connected (1, 2));
        System.out.println (t.connected (0, 3));
    }
}
```

Data structures that efficiently implement what we have called connect and connected are more generally known as union-find data structures. The union operation corresponds to our connect, and is so-called because it takes the union of the two sets represented by its inputs. The find operation, on the other hand, returns the representative of its input. Using find on two inputs e and f and testing for equality of the results would correspond to our connected operation.

Exercise 6.4   Is the following a valid implementation of connect?

```
public void connect (int e, int f)
{
  int eRep = rep[e];
  int fRep = rep[f];
  for (int i = 0; i < t; i++)
    if (rep[i] == eRep) rep[i] = fRep;
}
```

Exercise 6.5   Is the implementation in Listing 6.9 valid for towns? Explain. Ignore overflow of nxt when deciding on your answer.

Listing 6.9: Towns Implementation?

```
public class townsImp2 extends towns
{

  //Invariant: towns x and y are connected in links if and only if
  //rep[x] = rep[y]; [0..t-1] are the chosen towns;
  //all rep[0..t-1] are <= nxt

  int[] rep;
  int t;
  int nxt;

  public townsImp2(int num)
  {
    t = num;
    nxt = t;
    rep = new int[t];
    for (int i = 0; i < t; i++)
      rep[i] = i;
  }

  public void connect (int e, int f)
  {
    nxt++;
    int eRep = rep[e];
    int fRep = rep[f];
    for (int i = 0; i < t; i++)
      if ((rep[i] == eRep) || (rep[i] == fRep)) rep[i] = nxt;
  }

  public boolean connected (int e, int f)
  {
    return (rep[e] == rep[f]);
  }
}
```

Again, note how the form of implementation is based heavily on the operations required by the specification. If other operations were required, the implementation we have chosen may no longer suffice. In particular, imagine the specification associated a travel cost to each road between towns, and an operation minCost for returning the minimum such cost. Our current implementation idea would no longer be appropriate, since now the actual links between towns are important: we care not only that two towns are connected, but also how they are connected.

Exercise 6.6   What are some possible ways of implementing this enriched towns specification?

Chapter 7

Context-Free Grammar Recognition

Our purpose in this last chapter is to apply loop invariants to a larger development than what we have seen so far. Context-free grammars admit many nontrivial algorithms where invariants can provide insight and aid understanding. Here, we have chosen one particular algorithm — Earley's algorithm — for determining the recognition of strings by grammars. We begin by introducing the required background and concepts underlying context-free grammars, then explain an abstract formulation of Earley's algorithm. While we could argue correctness of this version of the algorithm with invariants, we instead give a more efficient realization of the algorithm (developed in [1]). We then use invariants on this algorithm to show that it does the same thing as the abstract version, and give a variant that proves termination.

7.1 What are Context-free Grammars?

7.1.1 Terminology

Context-free grammars (CFGs) are a powerful means for specifying the strings that constitute a given language. The concept of language here is similar to a natural language in the sense that some strings (called sentences) belong to the language, while others do not. The languages we consider here are nowhere close to the complexity of a natural language, however.

For example, consider the language consisting of only the four strings apple, banana, orange and grape. If you are asked whether or not a given string exists in this language, you can compare it with the strings you know are in the language to reach your answer. For example, apple is in the language but peach is not. Context-free grammars are a formal means by which we can answer this inclusion question. We can give a context-free grammar for this language as follows.

$$P \rightarrow ab$$
$$P \rightarrow aPb$$

Figure 7.1: Example Context-free Grammar

$$Fruit \rightarrow apple$$
$$Fruit \rightarrow banana$$
$$Fruit \rightarrow orange$$
$$Fruit \rightarrow grape$$

The word $Fruit$ here is called a nonterminal, because it does not exist in the language described by the grammar. The other words (such as apple) are called terminals, since they are part of the makeup of the language. Nonterminals assist in giving structure to the sentences in the language, as we will see in more complicated grammars. In general, we use capitalized words (or single capitalized letters) for nonterminals, and lowercase letters or words for terminals.

Each line in the above grammar is called a production. Productions consist of a left-hand-side (which must be exactly one nonterminal), a right arrow, and a right-hand-side (which may include terminals and/or nonterminals). Since we only have one nonterminal, the left-hand-side of each production must be $Fruit$.

Along with terminals, nonterminals and productions, we must have one nonterminal in all CFGs that acts as the start symbol. The start symbol is the starting point of all sentences in the language. If we cannot generate a sentence from the start symbol, it does not exist in the language. The start symbol in the current example must be $Fruit$, so starting with $Fruit$ is the only way to generate members of the language. We explain this process next.

Exercise 7.1   Give a context-free grammar that includes all one- and two-letter English words.

7.1.2   Derivations

A single derivation step begins with a string that includes at least one nonterminal, and replaces one such nonterminal with one of its right-hand-sides. If we begin with string α and zero or more such derivation steps yield string β, we say β is derived from α and denote this as $\alpha \Rightarrow \beta$. When α is the start symbol, all such β are called sentential forms; if β contains only terminals, it is a sentence.

To exhibit the idea of derivation, we introduce a more complicated context-free grammar. Its start symbol (and only nonterminal) is P, its terminals are a and b, and its productions are in Figure 7.1.

Note how the second production is recursive, in that it includes P in both its left- and right-hand-sides. It is this feature of context-free grammars that admits most of their flexibility.

Beginning with P, we can replace it by one of its right-hand-sides to determine some sentential forms for the grammar. For example, ab is a right-hand-side, so

P derives ab in one step. That is, ab is a sentence of this grammar. Alternatively, we can replace P by aPb, so aPb is also a sentential form (but not yet a sentence) derivable in one step. We can continue here, replacing the P in the middle with the second right-hand-side again, yielding $aaPbb$. Performing this replacement again yields $aaaPbbb$. We could continue in this way forever, yielding sentential forms consisting of a sequence of a terminals, a P, and a string of b terminals equal in length to the a part. At some point, we must replace the middle P with ab to yield a sentence. Specifically, we have that $aaaPbbb$ further derives $aaaabbbb$, so $aaaabbbb$ is a sentence of the grammar. Using only the symbol for derivations, we can succinctly show that $aaaabbbb$ is a sentence of the grammar as follows: $P \Rightarrow aPb \Rightarrow aaPbb \Rightarrow aaaPbbb \Rightarrow aaaabbbb$.

For this particular grammar, we can characterize the form of its sentences in a simple way. It contains all and only the sentences containing n copies of a followed by n copies of b, where $n > 0$. Using this description, we can readily determine if a target sentence belongs to the grammar. However, we cannot extend this reasoning technique to arbitrary grammars for two reasons. First, just giving a textual description of what a grammar does is not enough. We must prove that the grammar does indeed generate exactly the strings we have described. While this is not difficult for the current case, it becomes awkward with larger grammars. Second, there may not be a succinct text description of the grammar's sentences. In this case, we have no choice but to somehow consult the grammar directly, determining if a sequence of derivation steps can yield our proposed sentence. Doing this requires a context-free recognition algorithm.

Determining the valid sentences of a CFG has many practical purposes. For example, of importance to any compiler is the parsing phase, where the source code is read and analyzed according to its structure. It is at this step where syntax errors are found; such errors exist in any program that does not correspond to a valid sentence of the programming language grammar. Context-free grammars readily model nested (recursive) aspects of programming languages, including expressions and statements. In Java, we have while-statements and if-statements, whose bodies are composed of a statement. This inner statement, of course, can be another while-statement or if-statement, and so on. As a second example, context-free grammars have been used in natural language processing. We may use a grammar that approximates a language like English, then use it to determine if target sentences are valid.

7.1.3 ϵ-Productions

A special type of production, an ϵ-production, can be used in a CFG to indicate that a nonterminal has the possibility of deriving an empty string. These productions are required when empty strings belong to a grammar, since without them we have no way of including such strings. Additionally, they can often simplify the structure of grammars where they are not strictly necessary.

Let us modify the CFG of Figure 7.1 by removing the first production and replacing it with an ϵ-production. The resulting productions are in Figure 7.2.

$$P \quad \rightarrow \quad \epsilon$$
$$P \quad \rightarrow \quad aPb$$

Figure 7.2: Context-free Grammar with ϵ-production

Beginning with P, we can use the ϵ-production to conclude that the empty string, ϵ, now belongs to the language. If we instead use the second production, we can derive aPb as a sentential form. We can then use the first production, replacing the P with ϵ, to conclude that ab is a sentence. (An ϵ in a sentence adds nothing to its contents, so effectively disappears.) The language of this grammar is the same as that of Figure 7.1, except that it additionally includes the empty string.

By including ϵ-productions, we create the possibility of a nonterminal generating the empty string. Such nonterminals are called *nullable*, and play havoc with many naive recognition algorithms we might try. While they do cause problems in Earley recognizers, we can fortunately deal with them in an elegant way.

To appreciate the difficulties caused by ϵ-productions, let's start with a simple recognition algorithm we might expect would work in their absence. Assume that we are given a CFG and a sentence for which we want to determine derivability from the start symbol. One of the right-hand-sides of the start symbol must derive the entire sentence. That is, the first step in a derivation must replace the start symbol with one of its right-hand-sides. If a right-hand-side is $\alpha\beta\gamma\ldots$ and the sentence is $abc\ldots$, then α must derive some first part of the input, β must derive some subsequent part of the input, and so on. If this can be done, then we know that this particular right-hand-side can derive the entire sentence, and so too can the start symbol. The problem, of course, is that we do not know how to *partition* the input sentence among the symbols $\alpha\beta\gamma\ldots$. Since we do not know how to partition the sentence, we must try all possible partitions. If we are assuming that there are no ϵ-productions, this amounts to dividing $abc\ldots$ in such a way that $\alpha, \beta, \gamma, \ldots$ are individually "responsible" for deriving non-empty consecutive parts of the input. Assuming there are p ways of accomplishing this partition, we have p new problems to solve, all of which may require further partitioning. We can only stop this partitioning when we reach the level of terminals; if we are trying to ascertain whether one terminal derives another, we can answer this directly, without partitioning anything. This is because one terminal derives another only when they are the same terminal. The approach here is a classic realization of the depth-first search technique. We start with a problem to solve, break it into subproblems, and recursively solve those subproblems in turn. The recursion ends when the subproblems are trivially solved.

What happens when "subproblems" are the same as an original problem? In this case, we may end up requiring the solution to the exact problem we are trying to solve. This would cause an infinite recursion to ensue, and it can result if we include ϵ-productions in the grammar. For example, consider the following grammar:

$$A \rightarrow BA$$
$$A \rightarrow a$$
$$B \rightarrow \epsilon$$

Consider input sentence aaa. Is it a sentence of the grammar? To determine this, we would start with the first production of A, and partition the sentence in all possible ways among the two symbols of its right-hand-side. The only way this can possibly succeed is if we give B nothing (since it can only derive ϵ), and give all of aaa to A. But this again yields a subproblem of finding a partition of aaa for a right-hand-side of A. We will therefore try the right-hand-sides of A again, in turn. Thus, we will use the first right-hand-side again, making no progress as before. We will keep looping in this way, never making progress.

This recognition attempt was described by Unger [15]; the problems caused by ϵ-productions are well-known. One proposed solution includes maintaining a "subproblem stack", which we search through to ensure we never try to solve a subproblem that is already present. Alternatively, we may transform the grammar into a specific form so that its structure does not cause infinite recursion. There are normal forms for context-free grammars, such as Chomsky Normal Form, that prescribe a designated format for the contained productions. Regardless, we are faced with obscuring the recognition algorithm, the grammar, or both. This is a fact of life that has been faced over and over when developing recognition algorithms, and makes reasoning about their correctness or efficiency a complex task. The next section describes Earley's algorithm. By now it is no surprise that ϵ-productions will be troublesome, but the resolution is far more elegant than what is required by other attempts.

7.1.4 Parse Trees

Sometimes it is helpful to view derivations in a graphical format rather than as a sequence of strings connected with the $\Rightarrow$ symbol. We can use parse trees to visualize the means by which a string is found to belong to a context-free grammar. Of equal importance, parse trees often facilitate proofs of properties of CFGs, as we will later see when studying a nullability algorithm.

Parse trees are trees whose interior nodes are nonterminals of a CFG, and whose leaves are terminals, nonterminals or ϵ. If a node A has children $x_1x_2x_3\ldots$, then $A \rightarrow x_1x_2x_3\ldots$ must be a production in the CFG. If these conditions are met, any parse tree whose root is the start symbol and whose leaves are all terminals represents a valid derivation of a sentence in the CFG. Specifically, if we have a parse tree whose root is the start symbol and whose leaves, from the left, are $x_1x_2x_3\ldots$, then we have proof that $x_1x_2x_3\ldots$ is a sentence of the grammar. We call the concatenation of the leaves of a parse tree ($x_1x_2x_3\ldots$ here) the tree's yield.

Derivations and parse trees are equivalent in the following sense. Imagine we find a sentence to belong to a CFG via a derivation from the start symbol. Then, we can find a parse tree for the CFG with the start symbol at its root and this sentence as its yield. Similarly, if we have a parse tree with the start

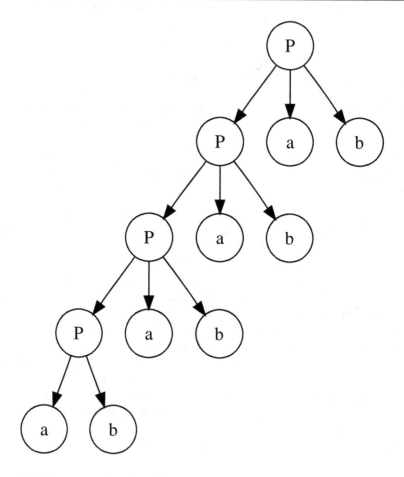

Figure 7.3: Parse tree for showing *aaaabbbb* is a sentence of the grammar whose productions are in Figure 7.1

symbol at its root and a sentence as its yield, we can exhibit a derivation from the start symbol that results in this sentence.

Parse trees with other properties are sometimes useful as well. First, a parse tree with *any* nonterminal N at its root and a yield of terminals s shows that s is a sentence derivable from N. Second, if the yield of a parse tree does not consist entirely of terminals, but includes some nonterminals as well, it represents a sentential form derivable from the nonterminal at its root.

For an example of a parse tree, consider Figure 7.3. It represents the fact that *aaaabbbb* is a sentence of the grammar whose productions were given in Figure 7.1. We saw this same fact in Section 7.1.2, but in the context of derivations instead of parse trees.

7.2   Earley's Algorithm

Earley's algorithm examines, from left to right, the terminals that make up the input sentence we are testing for membership in a CFG. It uses the concept of an Earley state (or just state) to remember information it gleans about recognition as it is executing. The states direct future execution of the algorithm and ultimately tell us whether the entire input sentence can be recognized.

Each state consists of three components. The first component is a production of the CFG, the second is a pointer to somewhere in its right-hand-side, and the third is an integer indicating when we began recognizing this particular production. If the third component has value 0, it means that we began recognizing this production before scanning the first symbol of the input sentence; if it has value 1 it means we began recognizing it before scanning the second input symbol, and so on. The second component points to the next symbol in the production that we must recognize. If the second component points after the last symbol in the production, we have successfully recognized the entire production.

Assume the input sentence is of length n and consists of terminals $x_1 x_2 \ldots x_n$. The algorithm creates $n+1$ sets of states $s(0), s(1), \ldots, s(n)$, one corresponding with each position in the input sentence, plus one initial state set.

There are several convenient representations for states. If we arbitrarily number the CFG productions with integers, and refer to the components of a right-hand-side of a production with increasing integers, we can represent a state by three integers. Alternatively, we can represent a state in dot-notation by giving a production with a dot in its right-hand-side, followed by an integer. The dot represents the second component of a state; it indicates where we are in processing the right-hand-side. An example of a state that could be generated by the algorithm on Figure 7.1 is $[P \rightarrow a \bullet b, 0]$. It refers to the situation where we have recognized the first symbol on the right-hand-side, using the first input symbol. The dot-notation facilitates the understanding of the algorithm's workings, so we will use it in the following description and example. Our later implementation will use the three integers representation, since they are more easily programmatically manipulated. In the following discussion, we also assume that the CFG has only one production with the start symbol on the left-hand-side; its right-hand-side consists of only one symbol. If a CFG does not meet this property, we can easily convert it into an equivalent CFG that does. We simply introduce a fresh start symbol with only one production, whose right-hand-side is the CFG's old start symbol.

Assuming that the root production of the grammar is $S' \rightarrow S$, we begin with the state

$$[S' \rightarrow \bullet S, 0]$$

in $s(0)$. We then continue applying three operations to the states in $s(0)$ until nothing further can be done. At most one of the three operations is applicable to a given state. These operations are as follows [1]:

$$S' \rightarrow E$$
$$E \rightarrow T$$
$$E \rightarrow E + T$$
$$T \rightarrow F$$
$$T \rightarrow T * F$$
$$F \rightarrow a$$
$$F \rightarrow b$$
$$F \rightarrow c$$

Figure 7.4: Expression context-free grammar.

SCANNER. If $[A \rightarrow \cdots \bullet a \cdots, j]$ is in $s(i)$ and $a = x_{i+1}$, add $[A \rightarrow \cdots a \bullet \cdots, j]$ to $s(i+1)$.

PREDICTOR. If $[A \rightarrow \cdots \bullet B \cdots, j]$ is in $s(i)$, add $[B \rightarrow \bullet \alpha, i]$ to $s(i)$ for all productions $B \rightarrow \alpha$.

COMPLETER. If $[A \rightarrow \cdots \bullet, j]$ is in $s(i)$, add $[B \rightarrow \cdots A \bullet \cdots, k]$ to $s(i)$ for all items $[B \rightarrow \cdots \bullet A \cdots, k]$ in $s(j)$.

Note how the *scanner* adds items to $s(i+1)$. Once we have reached the fixed-point of these three operations on $s(i)$, we begin doing the same on $s(i+1)$. If the scanner adds nothing to $s(i+1)$, and we are not yet in state set n, then recognition has failed. The scanner can be conceptualized as adding all states that have recognized one more terminal symbol from the input, by moving the dot one position to the right. If there is no way to recognize any more of the sentence, the scanner can do nothing. The predictor is responsible for expanding all nonterminals that we are interested in recognizing (i.e. those after a dot), by finding their productions and adding them to the current state set. The states that the predictor adds in this way have the dot at the beginning of the right-hand-side, since we have recognized none of the associated production. Finally, the completer's job is analogous to the scanner's, but on the nonterminal level rather than the terminal level. That is, if we have recognized the next nonterminal in a right-hand-side of a production, the completer notes this by moving the dot over that nonterminal. If the item

$$[S' \rightarrow S \bullet, 0]$$

is added to $s(n)$ after $n+1$ iterations, then recognition was successful, otherwise recognition has failed. Observe that the scanner is only applicable when a terminal follows a dot; the predictor is only applicable when a nonterminal follows a dot; and the completer is applicable on items where the dot is at the right end of a right-hand-side.

To illustrate how the algorithm works, consider the CFG of Figure 7.4. The grammar recognizes expressions made of the variables a, b and c containing operators $+$ and $*$ (addition and multiplication). For example, the grammar accepts expressions $a + b$, $a + b * c$ and a. (It is a good example of how context-free grammars can model programming language constructs.) Note that the

$s(0)$

$(a1)$	$S' \to \bullet E$	,0	Initialization
$(a2)$	$E \to \bullet T$	,0	Predictor (a1)
$(a3)$	$E \to \bullet E + T$	,0	Predictor (a1)
$(a4)$	$T \to \bullet F$	,0	Predictor (a2)
$(a5)$	$T \to \bullet T * F$	,0	Predictor (a2)
$(a6)$	$F \to \bullet a$	,0	Predictor (a4)
$(a7)$	$F \to \bullet b$	,0	Predictor (a4)
$(a8)$	$F \to \bullet c$	,0	Predictor (a4)

$s(1)$

$(b1)$	$F \to a \bullet$	,0	Scanner (a6)
$(b2)$	$T \to F \bullet$	,0	Completer (b1)
$(b3)$	$E \to T \bullet$	,0	Completer (b2)
$(b4)$	$T \to T \bullet * F$	,0	Completer (b2)
$(b5)$	$E \to T \bullet$	,0	Completer (b3)
$(b6)$	$E \to E \bullet + T$	,0	Completer (b3)
$(b7)$	$S' \to E \bullet$	,0	Completer (b5)

Figure 7.5: First two Earley sets for the grammar of Figure 7.4 using sentence a.

terminals are a, b, c, and $+$, showing that other symbols besides alphabetic characters can be terminals.

Now, consider Figure 7.5, where we produce $s(0)$ and $s(1)$ for the productions of Figure 7.4, operating on the (accepted) sentence a. We have named the items in the state sets; the second column indicates the operation and item name used to add the item in its row.

The algorithm begins by adding item $(a1)$ to $s(0)$. Since it has a nonterminal after its dot, the predictor is applicable to it. The predictor adds items $(a2)$ and $(a3)$. State $(a3)$ has a E after the dot, but all states that could be added by the predictor are already present. State $(a2)$, however, has a T after the dot, so the predictor acts on it to add all productions whose left-hand-side is T. These states are $(a4)$ and $(a5)$. State $(a6)$ is an example of a state with a terminal after the dot. The scanner acts on it to add state $(b1)$ to state set $s(1)$. This is the state that permits the algorithm to continue executing in state set $s(1)$ once it adds all states to $s(0)$. The rest of the execution is similar.

Of critical importance to the correctness of Earley's algorithm is the observation that we must keep executing the predictor, scanner and completer until no new states can be added to any state set. In terms of implementation, this would translate to a loop that continues executing until an entire pass of the states in the current state set yields no new states. This is inefficient and requires a means whereby we can effectively compare the state set prior to and after a loop iteration. The goal of the next few sections is to reason about an implementation that requires only one pass of the states.

$$
\begin{aligned}
S' &\rightarrow E \\
E &\rightarrow E + E \\
E &\rightarrow a \\
E &\rightarrow b \\
E &\rightarrow c
\end{aligned}
$$

Figure 7.6: Another expression context-free grammar.

It turns out that when grammars have no ϵ-productions, a single pass of the states in each state set does suffice. How? To begin, we treat the state sets as state lists which have a definite ordering of the states. When processing such a state list, we begin with the first state, and execute the correct operation (predictor, scanner, completer) depending on its form. We add new states to the end of the state list, and do not add a state if it already exists. We then move to the next state and process it similarly, until we reach the end of the list of states. We will not miss any states in this way; that is, if we go back to the beginning of the state list and pass over it again, we will not add anything new. When ϵ-productions come into the picture, we aren't so lucky in using this naive idea. We might miss adding some states on the first pass, and must keep looking over the states until nothing new is added. In general, the number of required passes is unknown, so we would rely on a scheme that detects when an entire pass adds no new states. In terms of efficiency and ease of implementation, this added complexity is undesirable. Before presenting a solution, it is helpful first to characterize the nullable productions of a CFG. With this knowledge, we will be able to show that a simple change to Earley's algorithm allows us to scan each state list just once. The next section deals with finding nullable nonterminals.

Exercise 7.2   Consider Figure 7.6. Is the language of this grammar the same as that of Figure 7.4? By using Earley's algorithm, show that the sentence $a + a$ is accepted by the grammar. Show that the sentence $a+$ is not accepted.

7.3   Nullable Nonterminals

The goal of this section is to use invariants to come up with, and reason about, an algorithm for finding the set of nullable nonterminals of a CFG. To begin, it is important to note that nonterminals can be nullable even when they do not have an explicit ϵ-production as a right-hand-side. As a simple example, consider the CFG in Figure 7.7. The nonterminals are A, B, C, D; the only terminal is a.

We can use the first production to conclude that A is directly nullable; we can do similarly for B. Now, is E nullable? It does not have an ϵ-production like A and B do. However, one of its right-hand-sides is AB, and each of A and B is nullable. That is, we can start with E, derive AB, then derive ϵ by replacing A and B, in turn, with ϵ. Therefore, E is nullable too.

$$A \rightarrow \epsilon$$
$$A \rightarrow A$$
$$B \rightarrow \epsilon$$
$$B \rightarrow a$$
$$C \rightarrow AD$$
$$E \rightarrow AB$$

Figure 7.7: Another CFG with ϵ-productions

Exercise 7.3   Is D nullable? Is C nullable?

To write a Java program that returns the set of nullable nonterminals of a CFG, we first need a way to represent the CFG's components. Instead of explicitly storing the CFGs nonterminals and terminals, we will rely on the convention that the nonterminals are the uppercase characters A, B ..., Z and the terminals are the corresponding lowercase letters. This also dispenses with any problems that might result from a user specifying a string as both a terminal and nonterminal; these sets must be disjoint. To represent the CFG's productions, we make use of a two-dimensional array g. Each row of g represents one production. The first column of each row (i.e. g[i][0], for suitable index i) represents a left-hand-side of a production, and the rest of the column represents the corresponding right-hand-side. For example, the row {'C', 'A', 'B'} represents the production with left-hand-side C and right-hand-side AB. We assume that only nonterminals are used as left-hand-sides of productions. Finally, we make the simplifying assumption that the left-hand-side of the first production is the start symbol of the grammar. This all amounts to being able to use a normal two-dimensional character array as a CFG.

As we noted, we cannot expect to find all nullable nonterminals in one step, since some of them may not have explicit ϵ-productions. We will thus use a loop that keeps iterating until we have found all nullable nonterminals — after all, this is what we want from our postcondition. If we store the nullable nonterminals we have found so far in nullable, we might try, as invariant, "*all nonterminals in* nullable *are nullable*". We could make this initially true by adding all nonterminals with ϵ-productions to nullable prior to entering our loop. Then, we can do some stuff inside the loop, terminate when nothing new gets added, and conclude some stuff. But what can we conclude? The "stuff" references were meant to imply that we'd better be careful, or we will not have enough information to conclude the postcondition. In particular, if we terminate the loop after an iteration that adds nothing new to nullable, we can only conclude that all nonterminals in nullable are nullable, and the last iteration of the loop did nothing. It is not obvious how we can additionally conclude that nullable includes *all* the nullable nonterminals.

It helps if we are able to say more after each iteration, instead of always claiming "nullable is a subset of what we want". One idea is to classify nonterminals according to "how long" they take to derive ϵ. Specifically, we can look at the minimum height of any parse tree with a given nullable nonterminal at its root

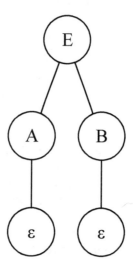

Figure 7.8: Parse tree for showing E is a nullable nonterminal of the grammar whose productions are in Figure 7.1

and ϵ as its yield. The height of a parse tree is defined as the number of edges on the longest path from the root to a leaf.

Consider Figure 7.7. The nullability of nonterminals a and b can be exhibited by a parse tree of height 1 by directly using their respective ϵ-productions. The nullability of E, by contrast, can be shown only by a parse tree whose minimum height is 2 (see Figure 7.8). If we can classify each nonterminal we have collected in nullable according to the minimum height of a parse tree that exhibits its nullability, we will be done when we can't add any nullable nonterminals using trees of greater height.

We will maintain a two-conjunct loop invariant. First, we state that change has value 1 precisely when there is at least one nonterminal that derives ϵ with a parse tree of at least height i. Second, we state that nullable contains exactly the nonterminals known to be nullable by trees with height at most i. Terminating the loop when change does not equal 1 then allows us to conclude that nullable contains all nullable nonterminals. The reason is that nullable contains all the nonterminals we can find with trees of up to height i, and change tells us there are no others we can find using taller trees.

The code listing for finding nullable nonterminals is in Figure 7.1. Note that the variable i we have been referring to is not required for program execution, but only used to facilitate the proof. That is, we could remove variable i and all statements it involves, run the program, and get the correct results. Variables like i are called ghost variables. (How spooky is that?) This is our first encounter with this type of variable, but they are often useful, especially when reasoning about concurrent programs.

To make the invariant true prior to loop entry, we set i to 1. Realizing that parse trees of height 1 can derive ϵ using only a direct ϵ-production, we must add all nonterminals with ϵ-productions to nullable. If we added at least one, change should get value 1. If we didn't add any, however, what should we set change to? Is there a chance that a tree of height ≥ 2 could show nullability of a nonterminal?

The answer is no, so we set change to 0 in this case. To see why, consider a parse tree T of height 2 whose root is shown to be nullable by the tree. The root's children, from left to right, are the right-hand-side symbols of a production of the root nonterminal. They all must be the roots of subtrees whose yield is ϵ, for otherwise the yield of the entire tree cannot be ϵ. Further, these subtrees have height 1. But, we already know that there is no tree of height 1 that yields ϵ. Therefore, there can be no such T of height 2 and, continuing with this reasoning, no tree of height $>= 2$ that shows the nullability of a nonterminal.

The body of the loop runs through each production, checking if each symbol on the right-hand-side has already been found nullable. If we find a production where this holds, we add it to nullable. These correspond to all nonterminals we can find nullable by using one new production, and hence all the ones we can find with a tree whose height is increased by 1. If we add anything to nullable during an iteration, we set change to 1 to reestablish the first conjunct of the invariant.

The termination argument for this algorithm uses two quantities, one of which must decrease on each iteration. First, if we enter the loop when change is 1, we decrease it to 0 if we find no new nonterminal to add. We cannot choose change as a variant, though, since on every other iteration it keeps its value of 1. We thus also use the number of remaining nonterminals that can be found as nullable, knowing that if change is not decreased, this value must be. The number of remaining nonterminals we can find is 26 (capital letters) minus the number we have found so far. Each iteration is associated with a positive value for the variant, since we do not loop unless change is 1.

Exercise 7.4 The variable change is an integer, rather than a boolean as might be expected. Why is this the case? Could we have used a boolean instead? If so, describe how.

Listing 7.1: Finding Nullable Nonterminals

```java
import java.util.*;
class earley
{

  public static Set<Character> findNullables (char[][] g)
  {
    //Requires: g meets conditions of CFG as described
    //Effects: returns the set of g's nullable nonterminals
    Set<Character> nullable = new HashSet<Character>();
    boolean allRHS;
    int i, j, change;
    for (i = 0; i < g.length; i++)
      if (g[i].length == 1) nullable.add (g[i][0]);
    i = 1;
    if (nullable.isEmpty())
      change = 0;
    else
      change = 1;
    while (change == 1)
    {
      //Invariant: change = 1 exactly when at least one nonterminal
      //in g derives epsilon with a tree of at least height i;
      //nullable contains exactly the nonterminals whose nullability can
      //be exhibited by a tree of height at most i
      //Variant: change + 26 - nullable.size()
      change = 0; allRHS = true;
      for (i = 0; i < g.length; i++)
      {
        j = 1; allRHS = true;
        while (j < g[i].length)
        {
          if (!nullable.contains (g[i][j])) allRHS = false;
          j++;
        }
        if (allRHS && !(nullable.contains (g[i][0])))
        {
          nullable.add (g[i][0]);
          change = 1;
        }
      }
    }
    return (nullable);
  }

  public static void main (String[] args)
  {
```

```
    char[][] g =
    {{'A'},
    {'A', 'A'},
    {'B'},
    {'B', 'a'},
    {'C', 'A', 'D'},
    {'E', 'A', 'B'}};
    Set s = findNullables (g);
    System.out.println (s);
  }
}
```

7.4 Earley and ε-productions

At the end of Section 7.2, we noted that, without ε-productions in a grammar, we can scan the states in an Earley state list just once to generate all new states. With ε-productions, though, we must check that we did not miss adding any states. To see why this happens, let us once again look at the three Earley operations.

SCANNER. The scanner adds new states to state set $i + 1$, while the predictor and completer are still acting on state set i. A key observation we can make is that running the scanner in tandem with the predictor and completer, or running it after the predictor and completer finish their work, is immaterial. The reason is that postponing operation of the scanner until after state set i is entirely constructed simply results in all items being added by the scanner at one time. If we run the scanner while stepping through the states in state set i, we incrementally do this work. The scanner, therefore, is not affected by the presence of ε-productions.

PREDICTOR. The predictor adds states that depend on the grammar's productions, not on the current contents of state sets. Thus, after running the predictor on a given state, later modifications can never allow us to predict anything new from this state.

COMPLETER. Once we run the completer on a state, can we ever execute the completer on this state at a later point to add new states? The answer this time is maybe. To see why, consider the completer acting on a state T whose third component is f. That is, it will be looking at state set f to find states whose dot can be moved over the next nonterminal. If $f < i$ (where i is the set currently being constructed), we can execute the completer once and never look back, since no state set prior to the current one can ever be modified again. Now, consider the case where $f = i$. Imagine we run the completer and add some new states to state set i. Then, further scanning through the states in state set i, we may add more states. If we then run the completer again on state T, we may have

$$S \rightarrow AA$$
$$A \rightarrow \epsilon$$

$s(0)$

(1)	$S \rightarrow \bullet AA$	,0	Initialization
(2)	$A \rightarrow \bullet$	,0	Predictor (1)
(3)	$S \rightarrow A \bullet A$	,0	Completer (2)

Figure 7.9: Naive list-processing Earley, failing to detect the root deriving the empty string.

created new opportunities for adding states. In other words, running the completer once was not enough to add all possible states in the future, because its operation depends on the current (and incomplete) contents of the state set being constructed. We seem to have found our problematic operation.

Figure 7.9 contains a grammar with an ϵ-production and the ill-starred progression of a naive list-processor not recognizing the acceptance of a sentence. The reason is that we could still use the completer on (2), using (3) to add

$$[S \rightarrow AA\bullet, 0]$$

to the list. We missed adding this state because we executed the completer to add (3), but did not run the completer again to take into account this new state. Recall that we want to run one operation on each state and progress to the next state, without looking back.

As we traverse a state list, our invariant must be strong enough so that we may eventually conclude that our list consists of all and only the states that would have been generated by Earley's algorithm. For all state lists after the first, we will begin by executing the scanner on the previous list to give us the "kernel" of the current list. Then, we process the current list in order, applying operations as we go, in order to end up with everything Earley's algorithm would generate. What are the required invariants?

As a first idea, consider an invariant that says that for each state we have processed, no completer or predictor operation can ever be used to generate new states. If we were able to maintain this invariant, once we had processed the whole list we would know that no Earley operation on any state in the list can be used to add any new states. But we already know that this is wishful thinking.

This proposed invariant can be maintained if we do not impose it on those states that are complete (i.e. there are no more symbols to process) and that have $f = i$. Let's call these states *bad states*. This eliminates the states that point to the current, incomplete state list, and hence are the only ones that can possibly generate new states at a later time. Note that states where $f = i$ but which are not complete do not cause a problem, since the completer is not applicable to them.

We can now weaken the invariant to claim that, among the processed states, only bad states can possibly be used to add new states at a later time. This leaves us the task of dealing with the bad states, since if we can account for the states they might add later, we would be done.

Consider a bad state T whose production has a left-hand-side of N. The key observation is that N must be nullable. The reason is that $f = i$, so we have processed the entire right-hand-side of the production without ever advancing from the list in which the state was originally introduced by the predictor. More specifically, we have not used the scanner at all for making progress through the right-hand-side of the state's production, so have done so without consuming any sentence terminals. Since N is nullable, any state that we have so far missed adding to the state list that could be added by a complete step on T has N to the left of its dot. This state must have been added by moving the dot over N in a state that already existed in the list.

Back to the invariant. For bad states, let us claim that (1) any state not in the list, but which can be produced by a complete step on a processed bad state, implies that the same state with the dot moved one position to the left already exists in the list. These states all have nullable nonterminals after their dots. Let us also claim that (2) if a state whose symbol after the dot is nullable has been processed, the same state with the dot moved once to the right has also been added. These two claims allow us to conclude that, after processing the whole list, nothing new can be added from bad states. All missing states imply that their "predecessor" states are already included and that their next nonterminal is nullable (claim 1); but we know that all successors of these states will be eventually added (claim 2). Combining these two claims with the earlier claim that all other processed states can never have any new states added from them, we can conclude that we have not missed anything.

We now see exactly how to modify Earley's algorithm; we must ensure that claim (2) in this invariant description holds. To do so, we check each state to see if its next symbol is nullable. If it is, we move the dot over the nonterminal and add the state that results. It is also important to check that doing this does not add any state that Earley's original algorithm would not have added, for then we may produce a set of states that is larger than the required set and therefore not the same. It can be shown by a proof on Earley's algorithm that we are indeed not adding anything that the original algorithm would not have added.

A Java implementation of this algorithm is given in Listing 7.2. It relies on the procedure to find nullable nonterminals given in Listing 7.1. Since we have not introduced succinct ways of referring to Earley states, in the interest of space we have left the invariants out of the outer loop.

The runEarley function first adds the basis element to the first (zeroth) state set. Then, we loop through all the state lists, each represented by a linked list in the array sLists. For each state list after the first, we first execute the scanner on the previous state list. Then, we loop through all items resulting from this scanner operation and execute the modified version of Earley's algorithm. That is, we execute the predictor or completer on each item; note the modification made in the predictor to account for incrementing j (moving the dot) to skip over nullable nonterminals. Once all state lists have been constructed, we return the truth value corresponding to whether the acceptance item is present in the last state set.

Exercise 7.5   How do we know the algorithm terminates? Specifically, exhibit a variant that shows we cannot infinitely increase the size of a state list.

Listing 7.2: List-processing Earley

```java
import java.util.*;
class earley
{

    public static Set<Character> findNullables (char[][] g)
      //find nullable nonterminals in grammar g

    //helper methods for classifying characters

    public static boolean isNT (char x)
    {
      return (Character.isUpperCase (x));
    }

    public static boolean isT (char x)
    {
      return (!Character.isUpperCase (x));
    }

    public static boolean runEarley (char[][] g, char[] sent)
    {
      //Requires: g is a valid grammar
      //Effects: returns true if and only if sent is derivable in g
      Set<Character> nullables = findNullables (g);
      int n = sent.length;
      List<state>[] sLists = new LinkedList [n + 1];
      state newState;
      for (int i = 0; i <= n; i++)
        sLists[i] = new LinkedList<state>();
      sLists[0].add (new state(0, 0, 0));

      for (int i = 0; i <= n; i++)
      {
        if (i >= 1)
          //scanner
          for (int inner = 0; inner < sLists[i−1].size(); inner++)
          {
```

```
      state curState = sLists[i−1].get(inner);
      int r = curState.r;
      int j = curState.j;
      int f = curState.f;
      int ruleLen = g[r].length − 1;
      if (j < ruleLen && isT(g[r][j+1]))
      {
        int nt = g[r][j+1];
        newState = new state (r, j+1, f);
        if ((nt == sent[i−1]) && (!sLists[i].contains (newState)))
          sLists[i].add (newState);
      }
    }

for (int inner = 0; inner < sLists[i].size(); inner++)
{
  state curState = sLists[i].get(inner);
  int r = curState.r;
  int j = curState.j;
  int f = curState.f;
  int ruleLen = g[r].length − 1;
  //predictor
  if (j < ruleLen && isNT(g[r][j+1]))
  {
    int nt = g[r][j+1];
    newState = new state (r, j+1, f);
    if ((nullables.contains (nt)) && (!sLists[i].contains (newState)))
      sLists[i].add (newState);
    for (int prod = 0; prod < g.length; prod++)
      if (g[prod][0] == nt)
      {
        newState = new state (prod, 0, i);
        if (!sLists[i].contains (newState))
          sLists[i].add (newState);
      }
  }

  //completer
  else if (j == ruleLen)
    for (int counter = 0; counter < sLists[f].size(); counter++)
    {
      state fState = sLists[f].get(counter);
      int r2 = fState.r;
      int j2 = fState.j;
      int f2 = fState.f;
      int newLen = g[r2].length − 1;
      if (j2 < newLen && g[r2][j2+1] == g[r][0])
```

```
                {
                  newState = new state (r2, j2+1, f2);
                  if (!sLists[i].contains (newState))
                    sLists[i].add (newState);
                }
              }
          }
        }
      return (sLists[n].contains (new state(0, 1, 0)));
    }
}
```

7.5 Conclusion

The previous examples in the book were simple enough that we could specify what we wanted from our algorithm within the text of the algorithm itself. For example, we can state in one line "find the value in the array" or "multiply the two numbers". Here, instead, we were given the specification of Earley's algorithm and worked to come up with a correct implementation. To be correct, we required the implementation to "do what the specification says". More specifically, we required producing the same elements in the state lists that were prescribed by the specification. To do this, we relied on invariants to guide the development of the implementation. The postcondition of the while loop is that we have produced exactly the elements that Earley's algorithm specified.

What we have done in this chapter is in reality no different than what we have been doing all along. The only difference is that, here, we had no easy way of specifying the implementation's postcondition. Indeed, such a postcondition would need to somehow restate Earley's algorithm, so that we knew precisely which states to add to the state sets. For this reason, and due to the amount of notation required, it would be unwieldy to include the loop invariants within the implementation. (Note at some points that we have triply nested loops.) More formal methodologies make provisions for specification and later implementation, and clarify what it means for the implementation to be correct. See Appendix B for an introduction to the B-Method, one such approach.

Appendix A

Supplemental Problems

The following are further exercises that can be solved with the help of invariants and variants. When not stated otherwise, they are fair game for the reader who has studied at least the first four chapters.

Throughout all the exercises, it's interesting to evaluate the effect of thinking in terms of invariants when writing code. For example, you may want to consider how you would solve a problem by "just coding", and whether invariants lead you in a different direction.

Exercise A.1   Listing A.1 contains a method for calculating the parity of a 32-bit integer. Parity is defined as the number of 1 bits modulo 2 in a binary representation of the integer. That is, if there are an odd number of 1 bits, the parity is 1; otherwise it is 0. For example, integer 8 in binary is represented as 1000; the parity is 1. The integer 15 is 1111 in binary; there are four 1 bits and so the parity is 0.

First, take a look at the code and try to figure out how it works. Then, give the precondition and postcondition for this method. Finally, come up with a loop invariant and variant and show that they are correct. Does your invariant clarify the operation of the loop?

Listing A.1: Parity of Integers

```
class parity
{

  public static int findParity(int x)
  {
    int i = 16;
    while (i > 0)
    {
      x ^= x >> i;
      i = i / 2;
    }
    x &= 1;
```

```
    return (x);
  }

  public static void main (String[] args)
  {
    System.out.println (findParity ((byte)8));
  }
}
```

Exercise A.2   The superincreasing knapsack problem [14] is defined as follows. You are given a list of integers in increasing order, which represent weights (in pounds) of the available objects. It is known that any weight in the list is greater than the sum of all previous weights in the list. You are also given a target value t. The goal is to choose a subset of the weights in order to arrive at exactly t pounds, or to report that this is not possible. Develop this algorithm.

Listing A.2: RC4 Initialization

```
class rc4
{

  public static void swap(int[] a, int x, int y)
  {
    //Requires: x and y are within bounds of a
    //Effects: swap positions x and y in a
    int temp = a[x];
    a[x] = a[y];
    a[y] = temp;
  }

  public static int[] initRC4 (int[] key)
  {
    int[] s = new int[255];
    for (int i = 0; i <= 255; i++)
      s[i] = i;

    int j = 0;
    for (int i = 0; i <= 255; i++)
    {
      j = (j + s[i] + key[i % key.length]) % 256;
      swap (s, i, j);
    }
    return (s);
  }
}
```

Exercise A.3   A fragment of the RC4 encryption algorithm [14] is presented in Listing A.2.

- The first loop initializes array s. Use an invariant and variant to characterize the contents of s after loop termination.
- The second loop uses the supplied key to jumble the elements of s. With the resulting s, RC4 proper can encrypt and decrypt a text message, using the same key for both operations. What can we say about the contents of s after the second loop terminates? Use an invariant and variant.

Exercise A.4   (Read Chapter 5 first.) An ascending segment is one in which each element is at least as large as the one to its left.

- Solve the problem of finding the longest ascending segment in an array using segment tables.
- Solve the problem of finding the longest ascending segment in an array by directly using invariants. This version should not use additional storage.
- Compare the two approaches in terms of speed, storage overhead and simplicity.

Exercise A.5   Given a string of decimal digits, write a program that uses a loop to convert its value into an integer variable. For example, the input may be the string 245; the output should be the integer 245. Include in your precondition any assumptions made on the format of the input string.

Exercise A.6   Consider the following sorting technique. Given input array a of length n, generate a random permutation b of the integers 1..n. Reorder the input array so that its first element is a[b[0]], its second element is a[b[1]], and so on. Then, test a for sortedness; if it is sorted, the program terminates (and you should go buy a lottery ticket). Otherwise, the process iterates again.

- Can you give a loop structure, including invariant and guard, that you can use to prove partial correctness of this sort method?
- Can you find a variant that guarantees termination?

Exercise A.7   Let x be an n by n array of integers. Write a program that will print the number of its first all-zero row, if one exists. Use a nested application of linear search [6].

Exercise A.8   An arithmetic series is a list of numbers, where each number results from adding a fixed amount k to the previous number. For example, the numbers $4, 7, 10, 13$ are an arithmetic series (with $k = 3$). A geometric series is one in which each number is obtained by multiplying the previous number by a factor of k. For example, $3, 9, 27, 81$ is a geometric series (with $k = 3$).

Write a program that determines if the elements of an array constitute an arithmetic series. Write a similar program for geometric series'. Are there any arrays that are classified as both types of series?

Exercise A.9   The Soundex algorithm is a phonetic encoder: it gives words that sound similar the same encoding. For each input word, it creates an encoding of exactly four characters: the first is a letter and the following three are numbers.

The first character of the encoding is the first letter of the input word. The numbers in the encoding are obtained from scanning the input word from left to right, starting at the second character. Each of the letters a, e, h, i, o, u, w and y are ignored. Each remaining letter is translated into a number and placed in the next position of the encoding, unless it would be placed to the right of the same number. (There can never be two equal numbers in a row in an encoding.) The letters and their translations are as follows: b, f, p and v are 1; c, g, j, k, q, s, x and z are 2; d and t are 3; l is 4; m and n are 5; and r is 6. If this process yields an encoding whose length is less than 4, it is padded with zeros on the right. As soon as the encoding is four characters, the translation stops.

Consider the word "dan". The first position in the encoding is d. The next letter (a) is to be ignored by the rules of Soundex. The final letter (n) has an encoding of 6, so the encoding so far is D6. Since we are finished scanning the word but do not have a four-character encoding, we pad it with two zeros, yielding d600.

- What is the Soundex encoding of the word "noon"? Find three other words that yield the same Soundex encoding. Do they actually sound similar? What is the Soundex encoding of "orange"?

- Use preconditions, postconditions, variants and invariants to derive a correct Java implementation that outputs the Soundex encoding of its input word. Be particularly careful with the loop guard.

Exercise A.10   (Read Chapter 5 first.)   The subset sum problem is defined as follows.   Given an array a, you are to determine whether or not some non-empty subset of the elements of a sums to exactly integer s. For example, consider a = {2, −3, 5, −1, 6} and s = −4. The algorithm returns **true** in this case, since elements {−3, −1} sum to −4.

- Can we ever return **true** when s = 0?

- What is the maximum s for given a that can cause an output of **true**? What is the minimum s?

- Come up with a Dynamic Programming algorithm to solve this problem. You will require maintaining a two-dimensional table of results.

- Solve the problem for sorted a. Is Dynamic Programming helpful here? How fast is your new algorithm?

Exercise A.11   Listing A.3 contains a method that is supposed to determine whether its supplied argument is even. Add a suitable precondition and postcondition. Annotate the loop with an invariant and variant to show that the postcondition is achieved.

Listing A.3: Even Numbers

```
class even
{

  public static boolean isEven (int i)
  {
    while (i >= 2)
      i = i - 2;
    if (i == 0)
      return (true);
    else
      return (false);
  }
}
```

Exercise A.12   Listing A.4 contains a method that is supposed to return the greatest common divisor of its two inputs. Add a suitable precondition and postcondition. Annotate the loop with an invariant and variant to show that the postcondition is achieved.

Listing A.4: Greatest Common Divisors

```
class greatestDiv
{

  public static int gcd (int i, int j)
  {
    while (i != j)
      if (i > j)
        i = i - j;
      else
        j = j - i;
    return (i);
  }
}
```

Appendix B

Invariant Tool Support

In the previous chapters, all of our assertions (preconditions, postconditions, invariants and so on) have been given simply as Java comments within the source code. They were useful as guides for developing our code (especially in the form of loops) and for providing documentation and facilitating understanding. But by virtue of being comments, they don't affect the running program at all. It is up to us to reason about our assertions, ensuring they hold when appropriate, and drawing only valid conclusions from them. Other programming languages, specification methodologies and proof assistants allow us to do more with assertions. Instead of limiting them to comments, we can often include them as clauses in code that affect the running program (or a proof of correctness of one). In this appendix, we survey how assertions (especially invariants) are treated in several programming languages and proof tools. We will see that the support for assertions runs the spectrum from completely unsupported and informal (Java) to completely formal (B, Why) and somewhere in between (Eiffel).

B.1   Eiffel

Eiffel [12] is an object-oriented language that shares many concepts with Java, including object creation via constructors, inheritance and polymorphism (allowing a variable of one class to hold a reference to an object that is a subclass). However, Eiffel goes further in providing support for class invariants, preconditions, postconditions and loop invariants.

As mentioned in Chapter 6, class invariants are properties that hold of all objects belonging to the class. For example, consider a class meant to represent a bank account. It will include a balance, and methods for depositing and withdrawing money. A possible class invariant is that the balance is always a positive amount, so that no accounts can be overdrawn. Class invariants are required to hold after a constructor is executed. Then, assuming the class invariant holds prior to executing a method, it must be shown to be true after completion of the method. These properties of class invariants are similar to those of loop invariants.

Class invariants are useful for showing the consistency of objects, since between method calls we know that the invariant holds. They are also useful for implementing methods, since each method can assume the class invariant holds on method entry. The tradeoff, of course, is that methods must reestablish the invariant prior to their completion.

Eiffel also supports preconditions and postconditions as part of the language syntax; they reflect what we have been using "requires" and "effects" Java comments for.

For a simple demonstration of preconditions and class invariants in Eiffel, consider Listing B.1 (a bank account class) and Listing B.2 (a test program).

Listing B.1: Bank Account Class

```
class ACCOUNT

feature {NONE}

amount : INTEGER

feature

deposit (value : INTEGER) is
-- deposit value into account
require value >= 0
do
  amount := amount + value
end

withdraw (value : INTEGER) is
-- Withdraw value from account
require value <= amount; value >= 0
do
  amount := amount - value
end

invariant
amount >= 0
end
```

Listing B.2: Bank Account Test

```
class TESTACCOUNT

create
make

feature
make is
```

```
local
a : ACCOUNT
do
create a
a.deposit (50);
a.withdraw (80);
end
end
```

The ACCOUNT class begins with a **feature** clause whose export list in curly braces is **NONE**. This means that all class features from here until the next **feature** clause are not available to be used by any clients of the class. (Features in Eiffel subsume the concepts of methods and data members in typical object-oriented terminology.) The only feature in this clause is amount, representing the amount of money in the account. We then begin another **feature** clause, this one allowing its features to be used by any client of the class (the default if there is no export list). Here, we have two features, deposit and withdraw, for respectively depositing and withdrawing money from the account. Both methods require their supplied values be positive, so we won't be able to deposit or withdraw negative amounts of money. Additionally, withdraw requires that the money being withdrawn not exceed the amount of money in the account. Finally, we have the invariant of the class, stating that the amount of money in the account is nonnegative. The class contains no explicit constructor, so an implicit one is used whenever objects of the class are created. Here, the implicit constructor will simply set amount to 0.

The purpose of preconditions in Eiffel is to specify exactly when a call of a method is well-defined. If a call is made to a method when the precondition does not hold, the method has no obligation to fulfill its part of the contract (i.e. establish any postconditions or maintain the class invariant). Therefore, when showing that a method maintains the invariant, we can assume on method entry that all of its preconditions hold, in addition to the class invariant. For example, we see that withdraw maintains the invariant because if its precondition holds, we will remove at most all of the money in the account, keeping amount nonnegative.

What happens when preconditions are violated? This corresponds to the situation where a method is called, but the caller has not first verified that the callee's precondition holds. This is a state we want to avoid, since what the callee will do when its precondition does not hold is not defined. Eiffel development environments will normally warn you of this problem with a "precondition does not hold" error. Indeed, this is exactly what happens when trying to run the test in Listing B.2.

It is interesting to consider what happens to preconditions and postconditions in the presence of inheritance. Imagine an object a is declared to be of class A. A central tenet of object-oriented programming is that, during execution, the reference attached to a can be an object of type A or any subclass of A. So, if code calls a method using the reference a, all it knows at compile-time is that it must ensure that the preconditions of the methods declared in A must hold. Specifically, it has no way of guessing the preconditions required by any subclass of A. If a is attached to an object of a subclass of A, then, calling code may unknowingly violate a precondition of a method. For this reason, preconditions are not allowed to be strengthened as we proceed down through inheritance hierarchies. For a similar reason, postconditions are not allowed to be weakened through inheritance links.

In Eiffel, we have runtime assertion monitoring. As programs execute, preconditions, postconditions and invariants are checked on-the-fly to make sure that they hold. If they do not, the runtime assertion mechanism can let us know via an error message or exception. What we do not have in Eiffel is a proof that our programs are correct. For example, imagine running an Eiffel program to completion without getting any "you broke my assertion!" errors. This doesn't mean the program is correct based on the specification. It only means that this individual run of the program set its variables in such a way as to satisfy all assertions. Regardless, it is a great help when assertions do not hold, since then we will be alerted to a problem area and can work further to determine what went wrong.

Listing B.3: Russian Multiplication

class RUSSIAN

create
make

feature{}

mult (x : **INTEGER**; y : **INTEGER**) : **INTEGER is**
require x >= 0; y >= 0
local
a, b : **INTEGER**
do
  from
    a := x; b := y
  invariant a * b + **Result** = x * y; a >= 0; b >= 0
  variant a
  until
  a = 0
  loop
   if a \\ 2 = 1 **then**
    Result := **Result** + b
   end
   a := a // 2; b := b * 2
  end
  ensure Result = x * y
end

```
feature
make is
do
  io.put_integer (mult (8, 9))
end
end
```

Now, let us look at Eiffel loop invariants and variants. Consider Listing B.3, where we multiply numbers as in Section 3.5. The mult method does the actual multiplying, and the make method is the one that will be executed when the program is started. We have a precondition and postcondition in mult, and also a loop with an invariant and variant. Eiffel loops include a **from** clause that initializes relevant variables, an **until** clause that gives the termination condition, and a **loop** clause that gives the body. Note that the loop continues *until* the **until** condition holds, not *while* a condition holds. The **Result** variable exists in all Eiffel methods that return a value, and **Result** is the value returned when the method terminates.

Operationally, Eiffel checks a loop invariant prior to loop entry and notes the value of the variant. After each iteration, the invariant is again checked and the variant is compared to its value on the previous iteration to make sure it decreases. Further, a check is also performed to ensure that the variant is always positive. Assuming all of these checks pass, no problems will be reported dealing with this loop. As with preconditions and postconditions, these dynamic checks do not tell us that our invariants and variants are correctly stated in the general case.

A general issue of Eiffel assertions (including invariants) is their restricted expressivity. Imagine we want to assert that a variable is the sum of the first i elements of an array. This cannot be expressed in standard Eiffel syntax and, with some minor adjustments, the Eiffel syntax is what we're allowed to use in assertions. One solution to this problem involves writing a boolean function, say sumOf, that takes parameters i, sum, and array a. It will iterate through the first i elements of a keeping a running total, then compare this to sum to check that they are equal. The problem with this "solution" is that we are essentially going to use the same code in the helper function as in the original loop. Also, we cannot check that the helper function is correctly running, or we'd require another invariant and some other helper function. If we are content to trust ourselves to write the helper function, we might as well go without the invariant in the original loop as well. ... but you've read enough to know this isn't happening!

The Eiffel assertion-checking facilities are a well-meaning step in the direction of correct software. Perhaps most importantly, they still "look like programming" and so are not difficult for most programmers to understand and begin using. More power requires more knowledge on the part of the programmer, as we will see in the following sections.

B.2   Why

Sometimes, we want to do more than Eiffel allows: we want to formally prove that our program will run correctly every time. One approach taken by the Why software verification platform [9] is to analyze code in a specific programming language and generate *proof obligations* (POs). These POs are what you would expect: invariants are preserved, variants are decreased, and so on. Why generates these obligations in a format suitable for proof by a *theorem prover*, or proof assistant. These tools may attempt to automatically discharge (solve) the proof obligations, require guidance from the user, or use a combination of both strategies. Regardless, once such a tool is able to validate all of the obligations generated by Why, the original program can be deemed correct.

Why can operate on several programming languages. It can directly operate on its own language, which includes arrays, loops, and other common constructs. With the use of add-on tools, it can also work with C and Java programs. We've seen our fair share of Java; here, we present some examples in C to give the flavor of how the tool operates. Why includes a program, Caduceus, facilitating the transition from C code to the proofs that must be carried out.

Let's begin with Listing B.4, an annotated C program for performing a linear search. Inside normal-looking C comments, we have directives such as *requires* and *ensures*, which impose preconditions and postconditions on the search function that follows. The postcondition says that, if the result of the function is a valid array index, it represents the location of the saught-after item v. Otherwise, if the function result is n, then there is no v anywhere in the array. The function body includes a loop, annotated with an invariant and variant, as expected.

Many provers can deal with the POs generated from this program automatically, requiring no input from the user. The proofs are straightforward enough that standard tactics of linear arithmetic suffice for most of the reasoning. For example, to show that the variant is decreased, we need to show that $n - i$ is decreased by the loop. Since i is incremented, this is easily seen to be true. As soon as we throw more complicated arithmetic properties into the mix, most provers seek human contact.

Listing B.4: Linear Search in Why

```
/*@ requires \valid_range(t,0,n−1)
  @ ensures
  @ (0 <= \result < n => t[\result] == v) &&
  @ (\result == n => \forall int i; 0 <= i < n => t[i] != v)
  @*/
int index(int t[], int n, int v) {
    int i = 0;
    /*@ invariant 0 <= i && \forall int k; 0 <= k < i => t[k] != v
      @ variant n − i */
    while (i < n)
    {
```

```
    if (t[i] == v) break;
    i++;
  }
  return i;
}
```

Listing B.5 is an annotated C program for Russian multiplication. The POs generated by Why cause most theorem provers to fail to prove many of the proof obligations. For example, they may not be able to deduce that dividing an even number by 2 and then multiplying the result by 2 yields the original number. One can get around this problem by adding axioms as annotations to the C source program so that they can be used by the theorem provers to help prove unsolved goals. Alternatively, one can use an interactive prover that allows the user to guide the proof and fill in details to allow the proof to continue.

Listing B.5: Russian Multiplication in Why

```
/*@ requires x >= 0 && y >= 0
  @ ensures
  @ \result == x * y
  @*/
int mult(int x, int y)
{
  int a = x, b = y, z = 0;
  /*@ invariant 0 <= a && 0 <= b && a * b + z == x * y
    @ variant a */
  while (a > 0)
  {
    if (a %2 == 1) z += b;
    a /= 2; b *= 2;
  }
  return z;
}
```

Note that we are ready to claim correctness of examples in Why exactly when we have discharged all of the associated POs. We are not running the programs at all and dynamically checking assertions as in Eiffel. In fact, since the assertions are given as comments, they have no effect whatsoever when the program runs. We are proving that no runtime assertion violation can ever occur, by virtue of discharging the required proofs beforehand.

Incidentally, how does Why deal with the binary search overflow of Section 4.2.3? By default, Caduceus will ignore potential overflow, so that theorem provers have no problem proving that potentially overflowing binary searches are correct. However, we can specify that Caduceus use a bounded-model of arithmetic (which is exactly what computers use, of course). When we try to prove the resulting obligations this time, we cannot do so, thus pointing to a problem.

B.3   B-Method

There are various formal development methods that allow one to begin with a specification of what a program is supposed to do, and arrive at a correct implementation of this specification. The B-Method [13] is one such approach.

B projects consist of machines that in turn consist of operations, data and invariants. We can think of a machine as similar to a class in an object-oriented language. As in Eiffel, each operation may assume the invariant is true on entry and must ensure that it remains true when it finishes. Operations may also include preconditions, restricting the conditions under which the operation may legally be called. Unlike Eiffel, B does not permit the postconditions of operations to be given. This is replaced by the concept of refinement.

Refinement involves beginning with a machine that specifies what we want to do, but not how to do it. For example, a machine that includes an operation for multiplying two positive integers has a body that effectively says "multiply the two positive integers". Any refinement of this machine is allowed to replace this multiplication operation, as long as it does the same thing as its abstract counterpart. That is, the postconditions of the two operations are the same. One valid refinement, then, is Russian multiplication: we know that it correctly implements the specification of multiplying two numbers. Another valid refinement would be using successive addition to effect the multiplication.

When giving our initial specification in B, we are not allowed to use loops. Instead, we use set-theoretic and logic concepts to abstractly specify what we want to do. We can, of course, use mathematical notions that are readily implementable as loops later. But, at this step we are more interested in modelling than implementing. When performing refinements, we move closer to what can actually be implemented in programming languages, until we arrive at B "code" that can be translated into a language like C. This process results in code that is correct by construction. More specifically, it is correct according to the abstract specification, since each refinement is required to preserve the properties of the operations.

Proving refinements correct requires discharging proofs. As with Why, some proofs can be discharged automatically, while others require humans to intervene. Tools are available for managing B projects and facilitating proof efforts.

Appendix C

Logical Basis of Invariants

Throughout the book, we have done much informal analysis regarding our programs and their assertions, invariants and variants. For example, we have argued over and over that our loops do indeed maintain our proposed loop invariants. Here, we show the logical underpinnings of this analysis. For further information, consult the excellent references at the end of this appendix.

C.1 Logical Connectives

In the following sections, we will focus on a more formal proof of Listing 3.3. To begin, observe again that the loop invariant contains three conjuncts. We have said that we must show that each such conjunct is established prior to loop entry, and that under the assumptions of the loop guard and entire invariant holding, we must show that each conjunct is maintained by one iteration.

In logical notation, predicates are separated by the symbol $\wedge$. A predicate is a statement that has a truth value (true or false). A conjunction $a \wedge b$ is true precisely when both a and b are true. For example, consider the statement "it is Wednesday $\wedge$ it is raining". For this predicate to be true, we require both that it is Wednesday and that it is raining. This (hopefully) corresponds to your intuition about invariants: each conjunct must be true in order for the whole conjunct to be true. A related logical connective is or; predicate $a \vee b$ is true when at least one of a or b is true. In the above example, if we replace $\wedge$ with or, the predicate would be true if today was Wednesday, or it was raining today, or if it were both Wednesday and raining.

We can write the loop invariant of Listing 3.3 as follows: $a \times b + z = x \times y \wedge 0 \le a \le x \wedge b = y$. Here, we have three conjuncts, all of which must be true for the entire invariant to be true.

The first property of this invariant we require is that it is true when loop execution begins. More formally, under the assumption that the precondition holds, we know that executing any statements above the loop results in the invariant being established. To represent the English equivalent of "under the assumption that", we use logical implication. We write $a \Rightarrow b$, read "a implies b" to signify that under the assumption a, b holds. We call a the premise and b the conclusion.

For example, consider the proposition "Today is raining $\Rightarrow$ school is canceled". For this to be true, we require that every time it is raining, school is cancelled. It does not matter what happens when it is not raining, for then our premise is not satisfied and the implication says nothing. In general, the only way an implication can be violated (made not to hold) is if the premise is true and the conclusion is not.

Another way to think of $a \Rightarrow b$ is by saying a is stronger than b. By "stronger", we mean that a holds at least as often as b does. For example, the statement $x > 3 \Rightarrow x > 2$ is true, because $x > 3$ is a stronger claim than $x > 2$: it is true whenever $x > 2$ is true, and also true when $x = 3$.

Claiming "under the precondition, the statements above the loop establish the invariant" can thus be realized as an implication. If we calculate the preconditions for which the statements above the loop establish the invariant, we require that the stated precondition is among these. Specifically, if we were able to calculate the weakest claim that a precondition must meet for it to establish the invariant, our stated precondition must be no weaker than this.

C.2   Weakest Preconditions

The weakest precondition of a program statement S to establish postcondition P is written $[\,S\,]\,P$. A weakest precondition is a predicate that must be true of any precondition in order to establish a given postcondition. If we state a precondition (in a "requires" clause), it cannot be weaker than the weakest precondition, for then it cannot guarantee to establish the required postcondition.

For example, consider incrementing variable x by 1 and trying to achieve a postcondition of $x > 4$. If our precondition is $x > 5$, are we guaranteed to reach the postcondition after the increment? We are, because if $x > 5$ and we increment x, we have $x > 6$ and so certainly $x > 4$. However, $x > 5$ is not the weakest precondition. We can pose weaker preconditions which hold in more states than $x > 5$, yet still guarantee to yield the postcondition. One such weaker precondition is $x > 3$. It is weaker because $x > 5 \Rightarrow x > 3$ or, alternatively, $x > 3$ is true in more situations than $x > 5$. This is in fact the weakest precondition: if we say any less than this, incrementing x cannot guarantee to reach the situation where $x > 4$.

Consider precondition P, program statement S and invariant Q. We require $p \Rightarrow [\,S\,]\,Q$: P is at least as strong as necessary for S to establish the loop invariant. For the program in Listing 3.3, this yields the following.

$x \geq 0 \ \wedge y \geq 0 \ \Rightarrow$
$[\{ a \ = x; \ b \ = y; \ z \ = 0;\}]$
$a \times b + z \ = x \ \times y \ \wedge 0 \ \leq a \ \leq x \ \wedge b \ = y$

Here, we have left out the variable declarations, and will assume that the variables have been declared appropriately. What we must do is calculate the weakest precondition for the three variable assignments so that we can reduce this implication to one involving only logical connectives.

Each type of statement has its own rule for calculating its weakest precondition. The rules we need here are those corresponding to assignment and statement composition, since we have three assignment statements in succession to deal with. To calculate the weakest precondition of the general assignment statement $[x \ = e] \ P$, the rule is to substitute all free occurrences of x with e in P. Free occurrences of variables are those that actually refer to program variables, and not "binder" variables such as the i in a statement like *for all* i, $a[i] \ \geq 3$.

We can use this rule to calculate $[x \ = x + 1] \ x > 4$. Substituting $x + 1$ for x in $x > 4$, we get $x + 1 > 4$ or $x > 3$. This, as we found before, is the weakest precondition for the increment to establish the postcondition.

For dealing with the composition of statements, we can work backwards, applying the assignment rule at each step, eventually arriving at the weakest precondition for the first assignment statement. We have three successive assignment statements, the last of which must eventually make $a \times b + z \ = x \ \times y \ \wedge 0 \ \leq a \ \leq x \ \wedge b \ = y$ true. If we apply the assignment rule on $z \ = 0$, we find that $[z \ = 0] \ a \times b + z \ = x \ \times y \ \wedge 0 \ \leq a \ \leq x \ \wedge b \ = y$ evaluates to $a \times b + 0 \ = x \ \times y \ \wedge 0 \ \leq a \ \leq x \ \wedge b \ = y$. This is the condition we must have prior to executing the third assignment statement, and this is equivalent to the postcondition we must ensure after the second assignment statement executes. We thus next compute $[b \ = y] \ a \times b + 0 \ = x \ \times y \ \wedge 0 \ \leq a \ \leq x \ \wedge b \ = y$, which is $a \times y + 0 \ = x \ \times y \ \wedge 0 \ \leq a \ \leq x \ \wedge y \ = y$. This is the postcondition that the first assignment statement must meet, so we continue by calculating $[a \ = x] \ a \times y + 0 \ = x \ \times y \ \wedge 0 \ \leq a \ \leq x \ \wedge y \ = y$, which is $x \times y + 0 \ = x \ \times y \ \wedge 0 \ \leq x \ \leq x \ \wedge y \ = y$. Simplifying this last predicate, we get $0 \ \leq x \ \leq x \ \wedge y \ = y$; this is the weakest precondition for which the three assignment statements will always establish the invariant. Thus, we are now in a position to prove that our precondition implies this weakest precondition:

$x \geq 0 \ \wedge y \geq 0 \ \Rightarrow$
$0 \ \leq x \ \leq x \ \wedge y \ = y$

We must therefore prove that, under the two premises, the two conclusions are guaranteed to hold. We can split this up into two smaller proofs, by focusing first on one conclusion and then the other. We thus first prove:

$x \geq 0 \ \wedge y > 0 \ \Rightarrow$
$0 \ \leq x \ \leq x$

If $x \geq 0$, then certainly $0 \leq x$ (or equivalently $x \geq 0$) must hold. The other proof, with $y = y$ in the conclusion, is immediate. It is this property of implications — allowing us to tackle each conclusion on its own — that lets us deal with multiple conjuncts of invariants separately.

In summary, we have shown that the precondition we gave for the program is correct in the sense that it is enough to establish the invariant of the *while* loop to follow.

C.3   Invariant Preservation

The logical proof that an invariant is maintained by the loop body is similar to the above. If the loop guard is E, the loop invariant is P, and the body of the loop is statement S, we must show $E \wedge P \Rightarrow [S]P$. That is, for the loop body to re-establish the invariant, it requires no more than the assumptions that the invariant and loop guard hold.

If we fail to prove this implication, it points to a problem in the loop guard, invariant or body. This happens when the premise of the implication is too weak to enable us to prove the conclusion. For example, imagine that a loop invariant is $x \leq 50$. If the guard of the loop is $x \leq 50$ as well, and the loop body increments x by 1, we cannot prove that the invariant is maintained. That is because our premise $x \leq 50$ is not strong enough to conclude $x+1 \leq 50$. We require a guard such as $x \leq 49$ — a stronger claim — to successfully reach the conclusion.

C.4   Further Reading

There are other proofs — including those related to variants — that must be performed for proving correctness. Schneider's book on the B-Method [13] is highly recommended for more information and examples on these types of proofs. Chapter 15 on loops is especially relevant, as is Chapter 3 on weakest preconditions. The B-Method is a formal method for specifying and implementing software, based on techniques we have studied in this book. You may find it interesting in its own right, but even if not, the syntax used by Schneider is similar to that used here.

A Method of Programming [8] is a classic book on programming by specification. It systematically introduces Dijkstra's guarded commands, which are conditional and looping structures that are more amenable to proof than the standard programming language variety. It gives further information on logic, and gives weakest precondition rules for reasoning about the new command set.

Bibliography

[1] John Aycock and Nigel Horspool. Practical earley parsing. *The Computer Journal*, 45:620–630, 2002.

[2] Roland Backhouse. Algorithmic problem solving. http://www.cs.nott.ac.uk/~rcb/G51APS/G51APS.html, 2007.

[3] Jon Bentley. *Programming Pearls*. ACM, New York, NY, USA, 1986.

[4] Robert S. Boyer and J. Strother Moore. MJRTY: A fast majority vote algorithm. In *Automated Reasoning: Essays in Honor of Woody Bledsoe*, pages 105–118, 1991.

[5] Thomas H. Cormen, Charles E. Leiserson, Ronald L. Rivest, and Clifford Stein. *Introduction to Algorithms*. The MIT Press, 2nd edition, 2001.

[6] Edsger W. Dijkstra. On a somewhat disappointing correspondence. circulated privately, May 1987.

[7] Edsger W. Dijkstra. *A Discipline of Programming*. Prentice Hall PTR, Upper Saddle River, NJ, USA, 1997.

[8] Edsger W. Dijkstra and W. H. Feijen. *A Method of Programming*. Addison-Wesley Longman Publishing Co., Inc., Boston, MA, USA, 1988.

[9] Jean-Christophe Filliâtre and Claude Marché. The Why/Krakatoa/Caduceus platform for deductive program verification. In Werner Damm and Holger Hermanns, editors, *19th International Conference on Computer Aided Verification*, Lecture Notes in Computer Science, Berlin, Germany, July 2007. Springer-Verlag.

[10] Yoshihiko Futamura, Chieko Shirai, Yongmei Liu, and Natsuhiko Futamura. P-segment tables : Data structures for programming problems concerning segments. *Transactions of Information Processing Society of Japan*, 38(6):1192–1203, 1997.

[11] David Gries. *The Science of Programming*. Springer-Verlag New York, Inc., Secaucus, NJ, USA, 1987.

[12] Bertrand Meyer. *Object-Oriented Software Construction*. Prentice-Hall, Inc., Upper Saddle River, NJ, USA, 2000.

[13] Steve Schneider. *The B-Method: An Introduction.* Cornerstones of Computing. Palgrave, 2001.

[14] Mark Stamp. *Information Security: Principles and Practice.* Wiley-Interscience, 2005.

[15] Stephen H. Unger. A global parser for context-free phrase structure grammars. *Commun. ACM*, 11(4):240–247, 1968.